Worry Workbook for Kids

WORRY
WORKBOOK for KIDS

50+ Fun Activities to Reduce Stress, Change Your Mindset, and Embrace Your Life

LAUREN MOSBACK, LPC, NCC

Illustrated by Sarah Rebar

ROCKRIDGE
PRESS

I would like to dedicate this book to my four wonderful children and to the amazing children and families I have counseled throughout the years.

For general information on our other products and services, please contact our Customer Care Department within the United States at (866) 744-2665, or outside the United States at (510) 253-0500.

Paperback ISBN: 979-8-88608-087-2

Manufactured in the United States of America

Interior and Cover Designer: Angela Navarra
Art Producer: Samantha Ulban
Editor: Laura Bryn Sisson
Production Editor: Jaime Chan
Production Manager: Lanore Coloprisco

Cover and interior illustrations by © Sarah Rebar with the following exceptions: © Robin Boyer: 7 right, 15, 25, 36, 37, 40, 80 left; © Joel and Ashley Selby: 27

10 9 8 7 6 5 4 3 2 1 0

CONTENTS

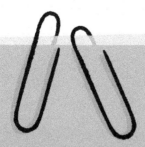

. . . .

Welcome, parents, caregivers, and therapists!

As a licensed therapist, I have worked with children, teens, and families for the past two decades. I have seen how excessive worry and anxiety can affect a child's life socially, emotionally, and academically. Also, as a mom of four, I know how difficult it can be to watch your child experience worrisome thoughts and challenging emotions. I am passionate about this topic because I have observed the transformation that can occur when a child learns the life-changing coping strategies found in this workbook.

Many kids worry, and if your child is experiencing excessive worry, you (and they) are not alone. In this empowering workbook, you will find 56 age-appropriate activities that are specifically geared toward helping kids develop the tools they need to cope with their worries. This book highlights a variety of evidence-based strategies and techniques proven to help address the thoughts, emotions, physical symptoms, and behaviors associated with worry.

Children will discover the skills they need to take a proactive approach to worry. This will include cognitive behavioral therapy techniques, mindfulness, self-care, exploring their individual strengths, and more! This learning facilitates the development of self-awareness, growth, confidence, and resilience.

This book is not intended to be a substitute for therapy, medication, or other professional mental health treatments. You can help support a child's growth by reading along and working through these activities together, as well as praising them for their hard work and effort. This book can be a great conversation starter!

Welcome, kids!

This workbook is made just for you, so you can learn how to let go of your worries! I'm a therapist for children, and worrying is the number one reason kids your age come into my counseling office. I'm excited to share with you the many ways you can overcome your worries.

Worries are unhelpful thoughts about the future or the past. They cause feelings of anxiety, fear, or nervousness. You'll learn more about this in chapter 1.

Everyone experiences worry from time to time. The activities in this workbook can help you cope with your worries in every part of your life—at home, in school, with family and friends, and out in the world! Through these activities, you'll learn various ways to retrain your brain to think more positively and to relax your body. With practice, you will learn how to transform your worries into happier thoughts and feelings.

To begin, set a goal. You can try one or two activities from this workbook each week, or maybe just pull out the workbook if you're feeling anxious or worried about something. You can do the activities in order or jump around. However you decide to use this book, it's important to try all the activities to get the most benefit and find what works best for you! And remember, if you're struggling, it's always okay to ask for help.

Let's get started by learning more about *you* and exploring lots of ways to feel calmer and more confident!

CHAPTER ONE

What Is Worry?

In this chapter, you can expect to learn what worry is, why people worry, what makes you worried, and how worry affects your body and your other emotions. You will explore and practice how you can live with uncertainty. You'll also learn how to use your own strengths to take charge of your worries.

UNDERSTANDING WORRY

A worry is a thought about the future or the past that makes you uncomfortable and that can lead to stress and anxiety. Here's an example of a worry that people might feel in a new situation:

David recently moved to a new town, and it's his first day at a new school. He worries about what it will be like: *What if no one likes me? Who will I sit with at lunch? What if I have to introduce myself in front of the whole class?* He begins to feel anxious. But once the day is over, David realizes it wasn't that bad, and his worry goes away.

Everyone experiences worry sometimes, and worry can actually be useful in some situations. However, extreme worry that happens a lot can start to affect your life in many ways. You could call this "Worry Mountain." This is when your worries and unhelpful thoughts pile up and grow so big that you feel like you can't overcome them. For example:

Zoe had a class presentation coming up. When she received the assignment, she started to prepare and get organized. Then, as the day of her presentation got closer, she began to have many unhelpful thoughts: *What if my face gets hot? What if my mind goes blank? What if everyone laughs at me?* Her stomach hurt and she couldn't sleep well. Now Zoe feels this way before every presentation.

With this workbook, you will discover several ways to confidently manage your worries, overcome obstacles, and shrink Worry Mountain.

WORRY SELF-ASSESSMENT

Circle whether the answer to the question is **YES** or **NO**. Fill in the blank when necessary.

Remember, there are no wrong answers! This quiz will help you better understand your worry, how to be more self-aware about what makes you worry, and how your worry makes you feel.

1. **Do your worried thoughts make you feel anxious, fearful, sad, or irritable?** YES NO

   → If yes, which emotions do you feel? _

2. **Do you play scenarios over and over in your mind?** YES NO

3. **Do you worry about what other people think of you?** YES NO

4. **Do your thoughts often begin with "What if . . . ?" For example, "What if something bad happens?"** YES NO

5. **Do you have a difficult time concentrating?** YES NO

6. **Do you avoid certain social situations?** YES NO

7. **Do you sometimes feel scared for no reason?** YES NO

8. **Do you have shortness of breath, sweating, dizziness, shakiness, stomachaches, headaches, or a hard time sleeping at night?** YES NO

   → If yes, which one(s) do you experience? _

9. **Do you wish you could stop worrying?** YES NO

10. **What do you worry about most?** _

    If you gave yourself more than one YES, this book was made for you! Let's go!

WHY DO I GET WORRIED?

You have worries for a good reason: Your brain reacts with worry, fear, and anxiety in response to possible threats. This is a natural response that has protected humans since the beginning of time. A long time ago, worrying allowed humans to be prepared for and survive everyday dangerous situations. People had to be ready to run from a predator or worry about where to find their next meal. Worry, fear, and anxiety allowed early humans to avoid dangers, survive, and evolve.

Although these exact problems might not affect you today, your brain can still react in the same way when it believes there's a threat, and this causes stress. When presented with a seeming danger, the body responds with the *fight-flight-freeze response*. This means your body is prepared to face, flee from, or hide from danger. Sometimes, this can help you—like motivating you to work on a school assignment. But most of the time, this biological survival instinct is no longer needed in your daily life. Some people worry when there is no problem and may respond to everyday situations as scary or harmful, even though there's no real threat. You can use the skills you learn in this workbook to fight stress and to help you identify when your brain is causing unnecessary worried thoughts.

IS IT REALLY A THREAT?

Decide whether each worry example below is a "Helpful Worry" or an "Unhelpful Worry." Circle the happy face if the worry is helpful or the sad face if it's unhelpful.

1. **You are on a walk when suddenly a dog walks toward you and starts to growl. You worry he might bite you, so you turn to walk away.** ☺ ☹

2. **You want to hang out with a new student at recess. However, you don't talk to them because you are worried they might not like what you have to say.** ☺ ☹

3. **You are worried about a math test that's coming up soon because you don't understand the material. This causes you to ask the teacher for extra help, and you do well on the test.** ☺ ☹

4. **You have been worried about your brother because people have been mean to him on the bus. You decide to tell your parents, and they help you problem-solve.** ☺ ☹

5. **You are worried about how you sound in class, so you never raise your hand even if you know the correct answer.** ☺ ☹

6. **You have a big presentation in two weeks and you feel a little anxious about it. This causes you to start the project early so you can practice in front of your parents.** ☺ ☹

7. **A friend rushes past you in the hallway. They do not wave or say hi. You worry that they must be mad at you. You think about it so much that you can't focus in class.** ☺ ☹

8. **A friend invites you over to their house. You keep having "what if" thoughts:** *What if I want to go home? What if my stomach hurts? What if I miss my parents? What if something bad happens?* **These thoughts keep coming, and you decide not to go.** ☺ ☹

Great job! Understanding which types of worries are helpful and which are unhelpful is a big step in managing your own worries.

1. Helpful; 2. Unhelpful; 3. Helpful; 4. Helpful; 5. Unhelpful; 6. Helpful; 7. Unhelpful; 8. Unhelpful

WHAT MAKES YOU WORRIED?

Many different things contribute to worry, such as a big change in your life, or if you're not getting the right nutrition and enough sleep. You might even naturally be a more nervous person. It's very common for kids like you to face worries about school pressure: things like homework, tests, and grades. It's normal as well to worry about social concerns: things like problems with friends, bullying, and peer pressure. Worries can also happen when you have too many things going on at once, such as when you're juggling schoolwork and extracurricular activities.

You might be worried about something in particular, like a test. Other times, you might experience worry but not be sure about what exactly is making you feel worried. You might just feel on edge. Living a busy and fast-paced life makes it difficult to slow down and really reflect on how you feel, why you feel that way, and what you can do about it. However, it *is* possible—and helpful—to pause and explore your thoughts and feelings.

You can learn to figure out the situations and events that cause you to worry. This will help you deal with them better when they come up. Becoming more self-aware will help you grow as a person. Take a moment and ask yourself: *What makes me worried?* Knowing what makes you feel worried is the first step in figuring out how to work through your worry. The next activity will help you investigate some of your worries and explore how much they affect you.

MY WORRY SCALE

On a scale of 1 to 10, where 1 is no worries and 10 is Worry Mountain, rate how much these situations do, or would, worry you. Then fill in your biggest worry.

→ Being left out by friends 🙂 ←①—②—③—④—⑤—⑥—⑦—⑧—⑨—⑩→ ⛰

→ Homework 🙂 ←①—②—③—④—⑤—⑥—⑦—⑧—⑨—⑩→ ⛰

→ Being away from parents
or caregivers 🙂 ←①—②—③—④—⑤—⑥—⑦—⑧—⑨—⑩→ ⛰

→ Tests 🙂 ←①—②—③—④—⑤—⑥—⑦—⑧—⑨—⑩→ ⛰

→ Someone is mad at you 🙂 ←①—②—③—④—⑤—⑥—⑦—⑧—⑨—⑩→ ⛰

→ Class presentations 🙂 ←①—②—③—④—⑤—⑥—⑦—⑧—⑨—⑩→ ⛰

→ Doing a new activity 🙂 ←①—②—③—④—⑤—⑥—⑦—⑧—⑨—⑩→ ⛰

→ Doing something wrong 🙂 ←①—②—③—④—⑤—⑥—⑦—⑧—⑨—⑩→ ⛰

→ Family arguments 🙂 ←①—②—③—④—⑤—⑥—⑦—⑧—⑨—⑩→ ⛰

→ Being called on in class 🙂 ←①—②—③—④—⑤—⑥—⑦—⑧—⑨—⑩→ ⛰

→ Being around new people 🙂 ←①—②—③—④—⑤—⑥—⑦—⑧—⑨—⑩→ ⛰

→ Getting sick 🙂 ←①—②—③—④—⑤—⑥—⑦—⑧—⑨—⑩→ ⛰

→ Certain animals or insects 🙂 ←①—②—③—④—⑤—⑥—⑦—⑧—⑨—⑩→ ⛰

Name your BIGGEST worry. It could be one from the list above or something entirely different.

- -

HOW WORRY AFFECTS US

Too much worry affects your emotions, your body, and your behavior. Common effects of extreme worry include having a hard time sleeping and struggling to focus. Worry can cause physical symptoms, too, like a racing heart, fast breathing, shaking, sweating, and stomachaches. People may feel tense, anxious, nervous, fearful, or grouchy.

These symptoms can feel overwhelming, but there are ways to reduce them. When you worry, think about how your body feels, what emotions you have, and how you act. These are signals that it's time for you to take charge! Ask yourself: *What is my body telling me? Where in my body can I feel my worry? What feelings am I having? What worrying thoughts are causing these feelings? What can I do about it?* For example:

Annica loves acting and is trying out for the school play soon. She doesn't know anyone in theater and begins to worry. Her heart begins to race, her stomach aches, and she has trouble focusing in class. She thinks unhelpful thoughts, like: *What if I freeze on stage? What if my mind goes blank? What if I don't even get a part? I'll feel like such a failure!*

To minimize these worries, she can remember that her body is sending her signals. She might think: *These thoughts are unhelpful and are leading to stress. I don't have any evidence these thoughts are true. Thoughts are not facts. I love acting and I'm good at it! I'm going to take a few deep breaths to relax my body and mind.*

MY BODY IS SENDING ME A SIGN!

When you worry, your body sends you signals in the form of physical and emotional stress. These signals let you know that it's time to reflect on what is behind that stress. This exercise will help you understand how and where you experience stress.

Look at the example below of common areas of the body where worry and stress can show up. Where in the body do you personally experience symptoms of worry?

On the next page, label where you experience physical symptoms of stress in your body. Next, on the lines provided, fill in the emotions and behaviors that come along with your worry. Finally, name a worry that might cause these symptoms or signs to occur.

Physical Signs

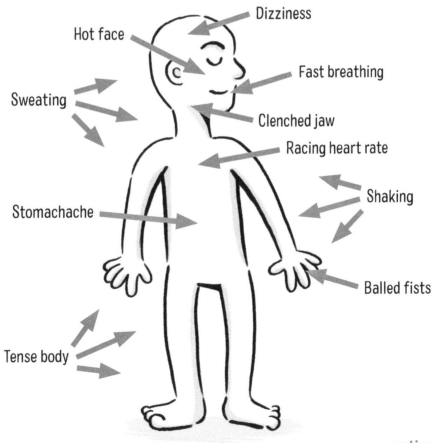

Dizziness

Hot face

Fast breathing

Sweating

Clenched jaw

Racing heart rate

Shaking

Stomachache

Balled fists

Tense body

continued →

My Physical Signs

MY EMOTIONAL SIGNS: (You might include: anxious, nervous, scared, grouchy, angry, frustrated, sad)

MY BEHAVIORAL SIGNS: (You might include: avoids certain activities or people, trouble sleeping, restless, anger outbursts, difficulty focusing)

What worry might cause these signs to happen?

LIVING WITH UNCERTAINTY

People often fear what they don't know. They might ask themselves: *Will this be a good or bad experience? Will I do well? Will I have fun or not? Will they like me?* People sometimes think that if they worry about something, they can stop it from happening.

Taking a healthy risk is doing something outside your comfort zone—something that you might feel unsure about. In general, healthy risks do not cause you harm. We all take small healthy risks every day. Examples of healthy risks include exploring a new place, trying new activities or foods, and meeting new people.

Even though you might feel uncertain about trying something new, it's good to take healthy risks. You'll develop new skills and confidence while lowering your anxiety and worries. Start taking healthy risks early on so you feel confident that you can take more as you grow. Doing something even if you're uncertain about it will help you prove to yourself that you can try new things successfully. To take healthy risks, you can follow these steps:

1. **Identify a worry.**

2. **Create a goal around this worry.**

3. **Break down your goal into small steps.**

4. **Take small steps toward reaching your goal.**

5. **Practice positive self-statements each time you take a step toward your goal.**

STEP INTO UNCERTAINTY

Review the steps below, then draw a line to match each statement with the correct step number.

STEPS FOR TAKING HEALTHY RISKS

1. **Identify a worry.**

2. **Create a goal around this worry.**

3. **Break down your goal into small steps.**

4. **Take small steps toward reaching your goal.**

5. **Practice positive self-statements each time you take a step toward your goal.**

A. Each time Sam takes a step toward his goal, he **WRITES IT DOWN AND PRACTICES A POSITIVE SELF-STATEMENT**. He says: *I can do this! I am brave. I am growing!*

B. Sam decides to **BREAK THIS GOAL INTO SMALLER STEPS** so he feels more comfortable going to the birthday party. He plans to talk to his friend Ben about the party, talk to his parents about how he feels, and practice climbing at the playground.

C. Although Sam is nervous, he really wants to go and have fun with his friends, so he decides to **CREATE A GOAL**. He says to himself: *Even though I'm nervous, I will go to the birthday party.*

D. Sam **IDENTIFIES A WORRY**. He is worried because he was invited to Ben's birthday party at a rock climbing gym. He has never rock climbed before and is unsure how it will go.

E. Sam puts this plan into action by **TAKING SMALL STEPS TOWARD REACHING HIS GOAL.**

A–5; B–3; C–2; D–1; E–4

LEAN ON YOUR STRENGTHS

There are lots of ways to lessen your worries or make them go away! Everyone has unique strengths and abilities. You can use these to help manage your worries. For example, you might be athletic and love sports, or you might love journaling, singing, or acting. Doing something that you are passionate about can be a great way to reduce stress and anxiety. Activities that interest you help you get your mind off your worries. Identify the strengths or interests that you can lean on to manage and overcome worry.

Example 1: Siddhant loves animals. When he is stressed, he likes to read animal encyclopedias or watch nature documentaries. This helps him feel relaxed and clears his mind.

Example 2: Camila loves gymnastics. When she is feeling worried and overwhelmed, she practices stretches and cartwheels. Exercise boosts her mood, and afterward, she feels more confident that she can tackle her worries head-on.

Example 3: Asher loves to read. When he is having racing thoughts and feeling anxious, cozying up with a good book helps him slow down his mind and body, which results in less anxiety.

Next Time . . .

I had a test today that didn't go well. I was so worried about it that I kept putting off studying, and I ran out of time. I feel so disappointed now!

Next time, I will study a little bit each night. I will use my passion for basketball and go shoot some hoops in the days before a test to reduce my stress.

MY SUPER STRENGTHS!

Think about the strengths you can lean on when you are feeling stressed. These could be character strengths, such as being kind, honest, or a good leader. Or they could be talents and abilities, such as being artistic, athletic, or musical. They could also be areas that you love and are passionate about that help you feel happy. You might love to bake, sing, color, or just be with your friends. Fill each star with one of your favorite strengths.

WHAT MOTIVATES YOU?

The things that are most important to you are called your *values*. They motivate and guide your decisions. Being able to identify your values and create goals around them improves your mental health.

EXAMPLES OF VALUES

PERSONAL: kindness, empathy, honesty, generosity

RELATIONSHIP: trust, friendship, family, loyalty

SCHOOL: accountability, teamwork, leadership, good communication

SOCIETY: sustainability, charity, social justice, environmentalism

To identify your values, it's important to also identify the hobbies or places that bring you happiness. For example, you may love being outdoors, so you may be passionate about preserving natural spaces. You can use these passions as motivation to overcome stress and worry. On the other hand, ignoring your interests may lead to more stress and unhappiness.

TIPS FOR IDENTIFYING YOUR VALUES AND INTERESTS

1. **Think about the examples of values listed on this page.**

2. **Think about the people who make you feel happy.**

3. **Think about the hobbies and interests that excite you.**

4. **Can you identify a goal or activity that would allow you to spend more time pursuing your interests and values?**

MOTIVATE MYSELF!

Read the example below and answer the questions that follow. Then answer the questions about your own interests and values on the next page.

Remy is passionate about art, but he spends a lot of his free time playing basketball because his older brother loves basketball. Remy loves being creative, and he expresses himself by painting and sharing his art with others. He likes spending time with his older brother, but when he's playing basketball, he usually daydreams about art projects. Whenever he draws or paints, he feels calm and joyful. If Remy has a bad day or is experiencing worried thoughts, basketball doesn't help him feel better. In fact, sometimes it makes him feel worse!

How does Remy feel when he's playing basketball?

- -

What is Remy's main interest, and what does he value?

- -

How does Remy feel when he does what he loves?

- -

What goal could Remy create based on his main interest?

- -

continued →

YOU!

What are some of your interests?

What are some of your values?

What is one goal you could create based on your values and interests?

How would you feel if you could work more toward this goal and do more of what is important and enjoyable to you?

LOOKING TO THE FUTURE

It is very helpful to identify goals based on your interests, values, and passions. **YOUR GOALS ARE IMPORTANT BECAUSE YOU ARE IMPORTANT!** Creating goals and taking steps toward those goals helps motivate you. You will feel stronger with the knowledge that you can make a difference. The confidence that you build can act as a shield to help protect you from worried thoughts and challenges throughout your life.

When you set goals, your focus should be on adding more meaning and value to your life. This approach is sometimes called having a growth mindset, which encourages more mindful and positive decision-making. When you have a growth mindset (which we'll talk about more later on), you know that with work, your skills get better over time.

So how should you start? It's helpful to begin by breaking down your ultimate goal into small steps—or mini goals—so you don't feel over-whelmed. Then, as you make progress toward your ultimate goal, you'll be able to celebrate each accomplishment, no matter how small! The progress you make will encourage you to move on to the next mini goal!

TIPS FOR SETTING USEFUL GOALS

1. **Reflect on your personal interests, values, and strengths.**

2. **Ask yourself: *What goal can I create to add more positivity and happiness to my life?***

3. **Create your goal, write it down, and divide it into smaller steps.**

4. **Brainstorm potential challenges and plan how you will address them.**

5. **Focus on what's going well. Celebrate each accomplishment!**

MY GOAL TO GROW

Fill in each blank with details of a goal you want to set.

My goal is _____.

I want to achieve this goal because _____

_____

_____.

I will achieve this goal [when?] _____

_____.

I will focus on these steps to achieve my goal:

Step 1: _____

Step 2: _____

Step 3: _____

What might stop me?

_____

_____

My plan to address that is

_____

_____.

WHAT WE'VE LEARNED

In chapter 1, you learned what worry is, why people worry, and how worry affects your physical body, your emotions, and how you act. You also learned how to tackle your worry by setting meaningful goals and using your unique strengths, interests, and passions. This information will help you in the next chapters as you continue to overcome your worry with your own power.

In this chapter, I learned:

Learning this information is helpful because:

So far, the most helpful idea or exercise for me is:

CHAPTER TWO

Challenging Your Worries

In this chapter, you will learn how to identify and challenge your worries. You will learn how to retrain your brain to think more positively and realistically, how to talk to yourself, and how to let negative thoughts go and practice mindfulness.

IDENTIFYING WORRIED THOUGHTS

Everyone has a lot of different thoughts throughout the day. We don't usually stop to notice every single one. Learning to become more mindful can help you identify your worried thoughts and make them better. Just like ocean waves come and go, so do your thoughts and emotions. When you identify your thoughts without judgment, you can ride along with the waves and find calmer waters. For example:

Natalie says to herself: *I just can't focus on anything! My best friends are mad at me. I just know it! I think they're whispering about me. What did I do wrong?* Suddenly, Natalie notices that her heart is beating quickly and her breathing is heavy. She also observes that her body is tense, her stomach is starting to ache, and she feels like she might cry. She thinks: *My body is sending me signals that my thoughts are causing me to feel this way. These thoughts about my friends are not helping me—they are hurting me.*

TIPS FOR NAMING AND OBSERVING NEGATIVE THOUGHTS

1. **Look to your body and emotions. Ask yourself:** *Is my body sending me any signs? What are those signs?*

2. **Notice what your thoughts are.**

3. **Write your thoughts down.**

4. **Ask yourself:** *Are these thoughts hurting me or helping me?*

5. **Remind yourself that thoughts and emotions come and go, and you will not feel this way forever.**

RIDE THE WAVE

Negative thoughts and uncomfortable feelings come and go, just like ocean waves. When you learn to observe and identify your thoughts, you are putting distance between yourself and your thoughts. This helps the thoughts lose their power. They are easier to accept because you realize they are not a part of you. They are just something you are experiencing right now. It's helpful to remind yourself that your negative thoughts in the past have come and gone, so these thoughts will, too.

Write down five negative thoughts you have had that have come and gone.

1. _____

_____

2. _____

_____

3. _____

_____

4. _____

_____

5. _____

_____

OUR STORIES

People tell themselves stories about lots of things—including themselves, other people, the future, and things they feel uncertain about. These stories affect how you view yourself and the world, but they aren't necessarily true. Stories may include your fears about things or comparisons to other people. It's important to remember that our stories are not always based on facts—even though they might feel true. Our understanding of events, other people's lives, and even ourselves is not always accurate.

Your inner voice is the narrator of these stories, and it plays in your head all day long. Some people refer to this as *self-talk*. Self-talk is often focused on the negative and can be unhealthy. However, when you learn to take control, your self-talk can be encouraging and motivating. You can rewrite your stories and turn negative thoughts into positive self-statements! With this small change, the way you look at life can change incredibly.

To identify the stories you tell yourself, ask:

1. *What stories am I telling myself about things that have happened in the past?*

2. *What stories am I telling myself about things that could happen in the future?*

3. *What stories am I telling myself when I compare myself to my friends?*

4. *What stories am I telling myself when I compare myself to people in the movies, news, or social media?*

5. *Are these stories helpful? What new stories can I tell myself?*

REWRITE YOUR STORY

Read how Paloma rewrites her unhelpful story. Then try rewriting your own!

PALOMA'S UNHELPFUL STORY: *I am never going to be good at math like Olivia. I just don't get it! It's too hard, and I'll probably fail the test on Friday . . . and every test after that. In fact, I'll probably fail math for the entire year and have to take summer school. I'm such a failure!*

REWRITE THE STORY: *I'm struggling in math right now, but it will get better! I'll ask my teacher for help after class, and I'll ask my neighbor who is great at math to be my study buddy. With a little work and extra effort, I bet each test will get easier and my grades will get better. I can do this!*

My Unhelpful Story: _____

_____

_____

_____

_____

Rewrite My Story: _____

_____

_____

_____

_____

WHERE'S THE EVIDENCE?

Remember, thoughts are not facts! Thoughts are mental events that pop up in your mind sometimes. They might cause you to jump to a conclusion that spirals into a bunch of worries for no good reason. When you are faced with a worry, try to gather clues and judge the evidence behind your worried thoughts. You can search for proof that your worry is true or false. Also, check in with yourself to see how you have been feeling. Did something happen before these thoughts started?

It's important to think *objectively* about the likelihood of your worry being or becoming true. Thinking objectively means you are thinking about something with an open mind—considering the evidence instead of your personal feelings. For example, if you worry that you will fail a test, think about whether you've actually failed many tests before. When worries build up, it can feel impossible to overcome them. And usually, there's no evidence to prove that your worried thoughts are actually true. The next time you have negative thoughts, be a "Thought Detective" and collect and compare evidence about whether your worry is actually helpful or not.

Each time you have an unhelpful thought, you can ask yourself: *Has this happened a lot before? Do I know this is true? Do I know this is a fact? What is my evidence?*

PUT YOUR THOUGHTS ON TRIAL!

In this exercise, you will act as a lawyer for the defense, a lawyer for the prosecution, and a judge to help you put a negative thought on trial. This will help you decide how accurate that thought is.

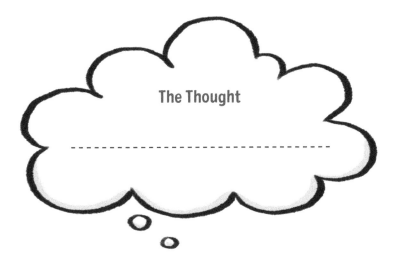

The Thought

- -

PROSECUTION: Gather evidence to prove your negative thought is false. You can only use evidence if it's a fact. No guesses or opinions are allowed!

DEFENSE: The same rules apply—only facts! This time, gather evidence that shows your negative thought *is* true.

JUDGE: Decide a verdict—or come to a judgment—regarding the thought. Is the thought fair and accurate or not?

THE PROSECUTION	THE DEFENSE
Evidence against the thought	Evidence for the thought
The Judge's Verdict	

I AM A THOUGHT DETECTIVE

EXAMPLE 1: Kaysan is playing baseball with his friends and strikes out. Even though he is great at baseball, as he walks away he thinks: *I am such a loser! My friends are probably laughing at me.*

1. **Underline Kaysan's negative thoughts.**

2. **What evidence proves or disproves those thoughts?**

    -

    -

3. **What is a more helpful and realistic thought?**

    -

    -

EXAMPLE 2: Vidya and her sister are trying on dresses for their school dance. Vidya shows her sister a dress she's picked out. Her sister smiles and says, "I love it!" Vidya thinks: *She's lying. I look terrible!*

1. **Underline Vidya's negative thoughts.**

2. **What evidence proves or disproves those thoughts?**

    -

    -

3. **What is a more helpful and realistic thought?**

    -

    -

CHANGING YOUR THOUGHTS

D id you know that you can change your negative thoughts by replacing them with more neutral or positive ones? It's important to remember that your brain likes to make more of the same kind of thought, so the more negative thoughts you think, the more negative thoughts your brain makes. The cool thing is that you can replace those thoughts and retrain your brain to think better.

For example, try changing thoughts like *I can't do this. I'm a failure.* to *I can't do this yet. I'll practice a little more and ask for help if I still don't get it.*

Or take a thought like *I know they're mad at me. I always mess things up.* Now try changing that to *They might be having a tough day. I can continue trying my best to be a good friend.*

And just like negative thoughts, the more positive thoughts you have, the more positive thoughts you create, and the better you feel! It's up to you to start retraining your brain to think more positively by rewriting your thoughts.

TIPS FOR CHALLENGING NEGATIVE THOUGHTS

1. **Spot your negative thought. Remember, your body will send you a sign in the form of uncomfortable emotions or physical symptoms.**

2. **Ask yourself: *What is the evidence that this thought is true?***

3. **Change your old thought to a new thought that is more realistic and positive.**

RETRAIN YOUR BRAIN AT HOME

Read the example below and fill in the blanks to change **THIS** to **THAT**.

THIS

OLD THINKING: *I know I won't be able to sleep well tonight. I'll stay up in bed thinking about all the things I'm worried about and never fall asleep. Then I'm going to feel so tired tomorrow. Ugh, why can't I turn off my brain?*

THAT

NEW THINKING: *I'm going to try a new bedtime routine tonight. I will _ _ _ _ _ _ _ _ _ _ _ _ _ _*

_ .

If I'm not tired, I will _ .

I will also try _ so I can

unwind and relax.

Try again! This time, read the example and change the thinking all on your own.

THIS

OLD THINKING: *I'm not looking forward to seeing my sibling after school today. They always annoy me, and then when I get angry with them, they blame me and tell my parents. My parents always take their side.*

THAT

NEW THINKING: _

_ _

_ _

RETRAIN YOUR BRAIN AT SCHOOL

Read the example below and fill in the blanks to change **THIS** to **THAT**.

THIS

OLD THINKING: *I can't do my class presentation today! I'm too nervous! I might freeze or say the wrong thing, and people might laugh at me.*

THAT

NEW THINKING: *I'm nervous about my presentation today, but it's _ _ _ _ _ _ _ _ _ _ _ _ _ _ _ _ _ to feel that way. I've practiced this presentation in front of _ and have spoken well in class before. I can do this!*

Try again! This time, read the example and change the thinking all on your own.

THIS

OLD THINKING: *My teacher asked me to stop talking to my friend in class again today. She said the same thing last week. Why does she always pick on me? She must hate me!*

THAT

NEW THINKING: _

RETRAIN YOUR BRAIN IN THE WORLD

Read the example below and fill in the blanks to change **THIS** to **THAT**.

THIS

OLD THINKING: *I have such a hard time meeting new people. I always get so quiet because I know I'll say the wrong thing. I'm worried about what people will think of me at camp this summer. Why can't I just relax and be myself?*

THAT

NEW THINKING: *Even though it can be hard to step out of my comfort zone and meet new people, I've done it before! Meeting new friends can be _____,*

and my friends _____. I'm excited for camp and meeting new friends!

Try again! This time, read the example and change the thinking all on your own.

THIS

OLD THINKING: *I'm not looking forward to our neighborhood picnic this weekend. I'm worried that I won't have anyone to hang around with and I'll be so bored. I already know this will be no fun at all. Ugh!*

THAT

NEW THINKING: _____

_____

_____

HELLO AGAIN, WORRY

How people react to their thoughts affects their stress levels and how their days go. Being mindful of your thoughts means you are aware of them as they are happening. When you notice, identify, and accept your thoughts, you can let them go more easily. Taking a mindful moment lets you recognize the thought, but also confront and maybe even disagree with that thought. For example, the next time you are aware that you are experiencing a negative thought, you could think, *Hi, worries, thank you for trying to help me, but I've got this. I don't need your help right now. Bye!* You can talk back to your thoughts in a calm way that takes away their power.

When you have negative thoughts, your body reacts and sends you signs in the form of physical and emotional stress. Once you learn the first step of recognizing your thoughts and how they are affecting you, you can then learn ways to release them. One way is through mindful breathing: Close your eyes, relax your body, and breathe out the tension and negative thoughts in your body.

Once you have put space between yourself and your negative thoughts, you can try to name something positive. It could be something simple, like *I'm glad I was able to recognize my negative thought today.*

LET IT GO!

Inside each balloon on this page, write down a negative thought that you have now or have had in the past that you'd like to let go of.

For example, you might write in thoughts like *What if I fail the test? What if I forget my lines during the performance? Do they like me?*

Fill the balloons with new, encouraging thoughts that you'd like to keep!

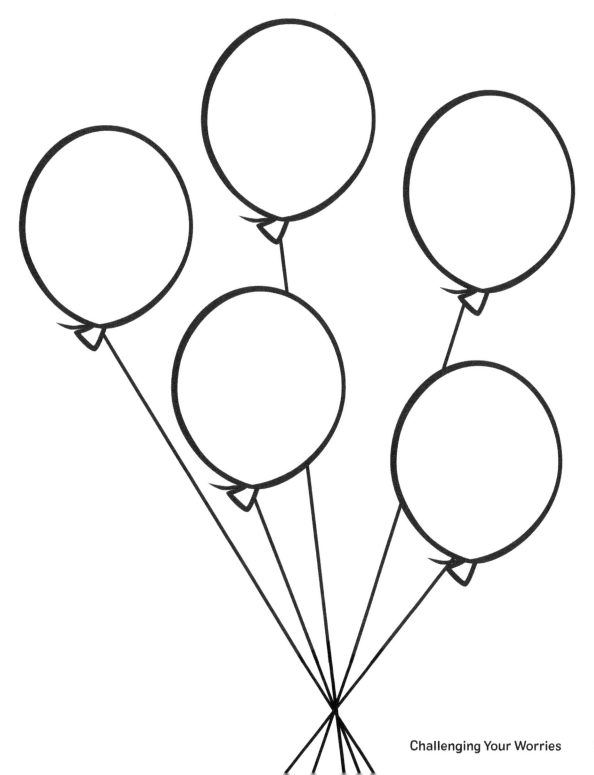

I THINK I CAN

Self-talk is the way you talk to yourself, or your inner voice. You can have positive self-talk or negative self-talk. Negative self-talk uses judgmental and blaming sentences, while positive self-talk uses supportive sentences.

Many people who experience worry have a lot of negative self-talk. This is discouraging and often leads to low self-esteem.

Take a moment to think about your self-talk. Are you critical of yourself? Or are you supportive of yourself? Do you say things to yourself like *I'm doing the best I can! I'm proud of myself for trying!* Or do you say things like *Everyone must think I'm stupid. I'll never be good enough!*

Positive self-talk is encouraging. It leads to positive feelings and behaviors. By using more positive self-talk, you are more likely to build healthy self-esteem, feel confident, overcome worries more easily, and take productive steps toward achieving your goals.

One way to start practicing positive self-talk is to use *positive affirmations*. These are positive self-statements that remind you that you are valuable and have many positive attributes to share with the world.

HOW TO USE POSITIVE SELF-AFFIRMATIONS

1. Begin your statements with *I am*, *I have*, *I do*, or *I can*.

2. Write down five of your strengths, talents, abilities, and/or skills you want to learn.

3. Repeat your affirmations whenever you think of them.

4. Repeat your affirmations whenever you are doubting yourself or having discouraging thoughts.

5. Repeat your affirmations daily while looking in the mirror, or close your eyes and imagine your affirmations.

Next Time . . .

I was asked to introduce myself to my new class today. I was so nervous and kept thinking, What if I freeze and the words don't come out right? What if they don't like me?

Next time, I'll reframe my thoughts to be more reasonable and will practice my positive affirmations. I will think, I CAN do this. People enjoy being my friend. I am brave!

YOU SHINE!

Practice positive affirmations by filling in the rays of the sun below with your many character strengths, talents, skills, and passions. For example, you could write in words like *brave*, *joyful*, or *caring*. Once you fill in the entire sun, practice saying your personal self-affirmations out loud. For example: *I am brave*, *I am creative*, *I am peaceful*, etc.

Remember the words you practice, and keep repeating them to yourself. It can start to become automatic, so practicing positive affirmations is a fantastic way to retrain your brain to think more positively!

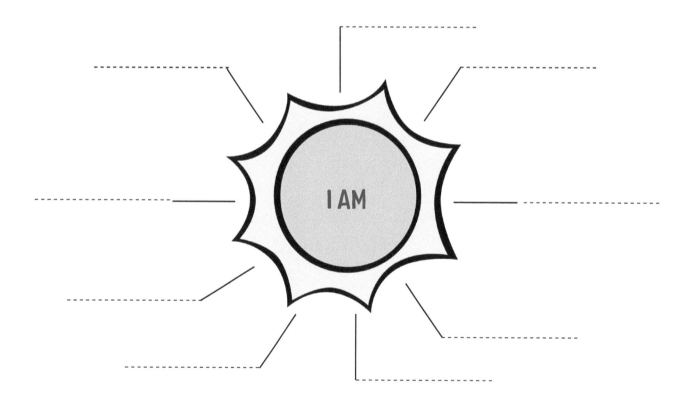

STUCK IN YOUR HEAD

Sometimes people focus on a problem or many problems for so long that they get stuck on them. This is called *rumination*.

Imagine thoughts being stuck in your brain like bubble gum on the sidewalk. The longer negative thoughts are there, the more stuck they get, and the harder it can be to get rid of them. Rumination is not a useful way to solve problems. In fact, it often creates bigger problems. When people ruminate, they have a hard time getting the negative thoughts out of their minds. Those thoughts end up growing bigger and multiplying, which causes people to feel worse than when they started thinking about what was bothering them in the first place. So when you notice that you are ruminating and your thoughts are getting stuck, it's critical to work on getting these thoughts unstuck.

TIPS ON GETTING UNSTUCK

1. ***Distract yourself.*** Call a friend, read a book, or draw a picture.

2. ***Challenge your thoughts.*** Ask yourself: Where is the evidence this thought is true?

3. ***Practice positive affirmations.*** Boost your self-esteem and remind yourself that no one is perfect. We are all works in progress.

4. ***Practice mindfulness.*** Go out for a walk in nature or around your neighborhood and explore your senses. What do you see, feel, touch, and hear?

GET UNSTUCK WITH 5-4-3-2-1

Practicing mindfulness can help you change your worried thoughts and get "unstuck." Instead of worrying about things that have happened or might happen in the future, you can try the 5-4-3-2-1 exercise. It can help you refocus on the present and feel more centered. You can practice this technique anytime, anywhere—at home, in school, even out in the world!

Look around you and name five things you can see, four things you can touch, three things you can hear, two things you can smell, and one thing you can taste. If there's nothing you can taste at the moment, name one positive thought. Write the things you named in the table below.

5 SIGHTS	
4 TOUCHES	
3 SOUNDS	
2 SMELLS	
1 TASTE (or 1 Positive Thought)	

WHAT WE'VE LEARNED

In chapter 2, you learned how to identify your negative thoughts, how to challenge your worries by looking for evidence to prove or disprove them, and how to rewrite the stories you tell yourself. You also learned about positive affirmations, mindfulness, and how to change your thoughts. This information will help you in the upcoming chapters as you continue to transform your worries.

In this chapter, I learned:

Learning this information is helpful because:

So far, the most helpful idea or exercise for me is:

CHAPTER THREE

New Ways of Thinking

In this chapter, you will learn how to better understand unhelpful thoughts. You will learn how to identify mental traps, how to problem-solve things ahead of time, how to avoid comparisons, and how to overcome the need for perfection. You will also learn what a growth mindset is and how to develop one.

IT WON'T BE A CATASTROPHE

Everyone has unhelpful negative thoughts from time to time, but those thoughts can multiply and trap you so that you cannot think clearly. These are known as *thought traps* or *stinking thinking*. You might believe that something bad is going to happen to you, that you might fail at something, or that something is wrong with you. The more you use stinking thinking, the more you will have unhelpful thoughts and unnecessary worry.

There are many types of thought traps. One type that causes worry and stress is called *catastrophizing*. A catastrophe is when something horrible happens, and maybe even hurts people, like a shipwreck. Catastrophizing is thinking things are much worse than they are and assuming the worst is going to happen.

Here is an example of catastrophic thinking:

I can't believe I raised my hand and got the answer wrong! What is wrong with me? My life is over!

Here is an example of helpful thinking:

It's okay to make a mistake. It's no big deal! Everyone gets an answer wrong sometimes. I am brave for raising my hand. I'll study a little more and get it right next time.

Catastrophizing is unhelpful because it leads to worry, stress, and anxiety. The amazing thing is that once you identify your thought traps, you become self-aware and can replace your negative thoughts with helpful ones.

TIPS FOR REDUCING CATASTROPHIC THINKING

1. Ask yourself questions: *What caused my thoughts? Do these thoughts hurt me or help me? What evidence do I have that these thoughts are or will become true?*

2. Write your thoughts down and change them to more positive ones.

3. Journal about your thoughts and feelings.

4. Talk to a trusted adult when negative thoughts arise.

5. Practice mindfulness to help bring yourself to the present moment. Breathe deeply or sing a song.

PRACTICE SHRINKING YOUR STINKING THINKING!

Free yourself from thought traps by shrinking your stinking thinking. Once you practice identifying your thought traps, you can use these strategies with any negative thought that comes your way!

Examples:

1. *I'll never be good at soccer.*

2. *What if I trip and everyone laughs?*

3. *I'm going to fail this test.*

Now fill in 4 and 5 with examples of your own thought traps.

4. _____.

5. _____.

Choose one of your thought traps from above, write it below, then answer the following questions.

_____

What is the worst thing that could happen?

_____

Do you have any evidence this will happen?

_____

How would you feel?

What would you need to feel okay in this situation?

What is the best thing that could happen?

How would you feel?

What is the most realistic thing that could happen?

How would you feel?

ALL-OR-NOTHING THINKING

Another thought trap that can cause stress and worry is called *all-or-nothing thinking*. This is when you view things as either all good or all bad, with nothing in between. All-or-nothing thinking can cause stress and worry when your thoughts focus mainly on the extremes or possible negative results. If you use these words often, it may indicate that you are dealing with this type of thought trap: *always, impossible, perfect, never, should, only, ruined, failure, disaster*. For example, saying, "Things never go my way!" is an example of all-or-nothing thinking.

Thinking in extremes is unhelpful because you might feel you must make either/or choices, when in fact there are many options in between. For example, you might have an unrealistic view that you or others are either wonderful or awful. These extreme thoughts can also make it difficult to complete your work, forgive yourself, and work with others. This results in poor physical and emotional health.

Things are not all good or all bad. Life is filled with *in-betweens*. Finding a middle ground is important, and to do so, you can learn to use *in-between thinking*. For example, all-or-nothing thinking might say, "There is only one way to learn art." In-between thinking would say instead, "There are many ways to learn art."

THE POSSIBILITIES ARE ENDLESS

Often, all-or-nothing thinking comes from focusing on only one thought and not thinking of other perspectives. One way to challenge this type of thinking is to come up with other possibilities for a particular situation that you are worried about, while focusing on more positive or neutral thoughts. This lets you practice in-between thinking.

Read the following example and list five other possible reasons why this situation could have occurred.

Your friend canceled plans with you at the last minute and did not give an explanation. You immediately think, *My friend doesn't want to spend time with me.*

List five other possible reasons your friend might have canceled.

1. _____

   _____

2. _____

   _____

3. _____

   _____

4. _____

   _____

5. _____

   _____

MIND READING

There are many forms of stinking thinking that trap us into thinking negatively. One of these thought traps is known as *mind reading*. Mind reading is when you believe that you know what others are thinking and assume that they are thinking the worst.

Here are a couple of examples of mind reading:

Why are they laughing? They must be making fun of me behind my back.

Why doesn't he want to play basketball today? He must be bored of hanging out with me, or maybe he thinks I'm terrible at basketball.

The reality is that no one can read minds. You can't truly know what someone else is thinking unless they tell you. The problem with mind reading is that it makes you feel insecure and uncomfortable around others for no reason. And these thoughts may cause you to act in a way that actually *creates* the situation you have been worrying about!

For example, if you think someone doesn't like you and you act as if they don't, they might pull away from you. You might think this proves your first negative thought, but it was never actually true in the first place!

THE THOUGHT-FEELING-ACTION TRIANGLE

The thought-feeling-action triangle below shows how your thoughts influence your feelings, which then influence your actions.

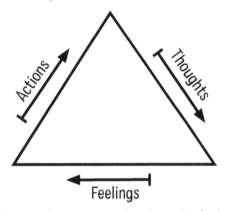

See the example below on how to put the thought-feeling-action triangle into practice.

SITUATION: You gave a presentation in class but stumbled over some of the words.

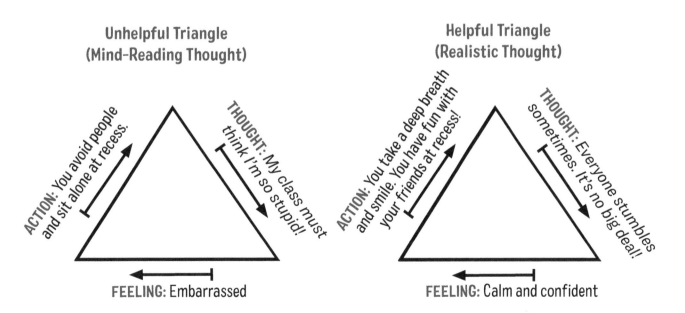

**Unhelpful Triangle
(Mind-Reading Thought)**

ACTION: You avoid people and sit alone at recess.

THOUGHT: My class must think I'm so stupid!

FEELING: Embarrassed

**Helpful Triangle
(Realistic Thought)**

ACTION: You take a deep breath and smile. You have fun with your friends at recess!

THOUGHT: Everyone stumbles sometimes. It's no big deal!

FEELING: Calm and confident

continued →

Now it's your turn to try! Read the situation and unhelpful triangle on this page and then create your own helpful triangle for it.

SITUATION: Your friend rushes by you in the hall without saying hi.

Unhelpful Triangle

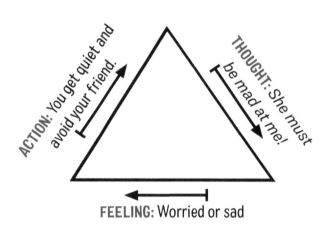

ACTION: You get quiet and avoid your friend.

THOUGHT: She must be mad at me!

FEELING: Worried or sad

Helpful Triangle

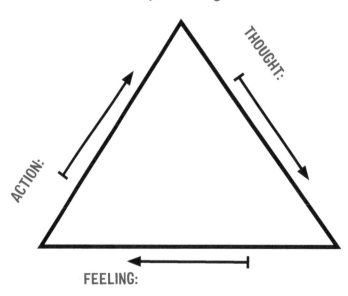

ACTION:

THOUGHT:

FEELING:

PERSONALIZATION

Personalization is another common thought trap. This thought trap occurs when you believe that an event or another person's negative behaviors are your fault or the result of something you did—even though they have nothing to do with you at all. Personalization can cause you to experience emotional distress. For example:

Liam is angry when he comes home from school. He ignores his younger brother, Aiden, and gets into an argument with his parents. Aiden sees this and wonders if Liam is mad at him or if he did something to contribute to Liam's anger. However, Aiden doesn't know that Liam's mood is because he has a lot of math homework and he's struggling with math at school. Liam's anger has nothing to do with Aiden, but in Aiden's mind, he's somehow to blame for Liam's bad mood. Aiden is personalizing Liam's mood, which causes Aiden to feel anxious and sad.

Have you ever assumed that someone's negative actions were because of you or something you did? Have you blamed yourself for situations beyond your control or taken responsibility for someone else's feelings? How can you work through this type of thought trap?

Once you understand the different types of thought traps, it's easier to catch the thoughts in the moment and avoid the trap. You can ask yourself: *Am I really the cause of this person's thinking or feelings? What is the evidence that my thought is true?* This thought process will help you avoid this thought trap and also allows you to have more empathy for others.

THE PERSONALIZER

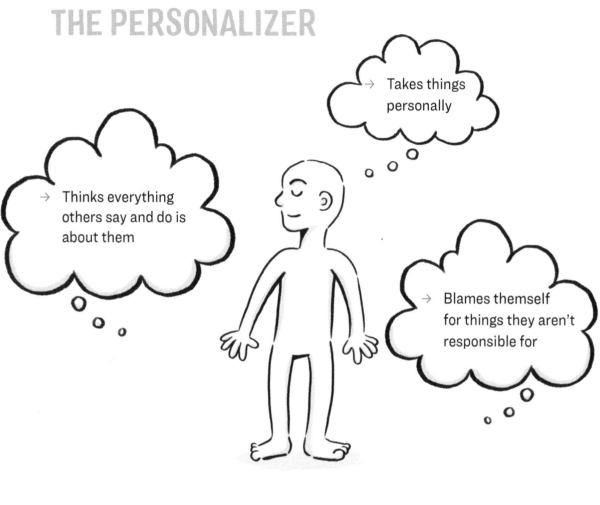

→ Takes things personally

→ Thinks everything others say and do is about them

→ Blames themself for things they aren't responsible for

How do you think these thoughts make the Personalizer FEEL?

How do you think these thoughts make the Personalizer ACT?

What are a couple of thoughts that could help the Personalizer feel and act better?

PROBLEM-SOLVING TIPS

The purpose of worry is to draw your attention to something potentially negative that might happen in the future. Worry arises so you can avoid physical or emotional discomfort. Staying safe and healthy is important, but there are more productive ways to ensure that you are staying safe and healthy. Too often, people react to their mental health and only practice coping skills once their worrying and stress have already started, instead of being proactive and working to solve the problem before it starts. However, it's really useful to take a hands-on approach to your well-being to get in front of your worry. The best way to do this is to practice self-care each day. This helps prevent your worries from turning into Worry Mountain, which often feels too hard to climb.

TIPS FOR PROBLEM-SOLVING WORRY

→ If your worrying has begun, ask yourself: *What is causing my worry? What am I trying to protect myself from?*

→ Identify your uncomfortable thoughts and feelings. Name how they are affecting you physically and emotionally. By simply naming them, you can get a better hold on them.

→ Next, explore and practice coping skills that work best for you.

→ Set aside time each day to practice a coping skill or self-care strategy when you're stressed and even when you're not stressed. This helps you become more resilient and can also prevent or minimize stress before it begins!

HOW CAN YOU PRACTICE SELF-CARE?

Self-care is taking care of your body (physical), your feelings (emotional), and your mind (mental). Self-care is taking care of the *whole you*!

You can practice this super skill in many ways. When you eat healthy, practice good hygiene, exercise, read, make art, talk about your feelings, or take time to rest and relax, you are practicing good self-care!

Color the rectangles with strategies that you already do in **BLUE**. Color the ones you would like to try in GREEN!

Do yoga	Read	Deep breathing	Dance	Exercise
Talk to a trusted adult	Make art	Play an instrument	Practice gratitude	Play a sport
Sing	Journal	List your special traits	Eat healthy foods	Stretch
Practice good hygiene	Get enough sleep	Be kind to yourself	Play with friends	Act/theater
Stay hydrated	Repeat affirmations	Take a relaxing bath	Walk in nature	Talk to a therapist/ counselor

When you learn to practice self-care techniques daily, you discover that you have the power within you to overcome difficult thoughts, feelings, and situations.

List two ways you can practice **PHYSICAL** self-care.
(Examples: Practice good hygiene, eat well, stay hydrated, exercise, get enough sleep)

- -

- -

List two ways you can practice **MENTAL** self-care.
(Examples: Read a book, listen to music, screen-free time, meditate, practice gratitude)

- -

- -

List two ways you can practice **EMOTIONAL** self-care.
(Examples: Identify your feelings, journal, talk to a therapist/counselor, create art, practice affirmations)

- -

- -

THE INCREDIBLE GROWTH MINDSET

Having a *growth mindset* means that you enjoy learning new things and view challenges with excitement. People with a growth mindset believe that their abilities can be developed with hard work. This view creates resilience and a love of learning.

A *fixed mindset* is the opposite of a growth mindset. People with a fixed mindset believe their abilities, talents, intelligence, and personality traits are unchangeable.

People with a growth mindset tend to be happier and achieve more than those with a fixed mindset. They might say things like:

→ "It's never too late to learn."
→ "No one is perfect. We are all works in progress."
→ "This isn't a failure. It is a learning experience."
→ "I learn something even if I make a mistake."
→ "Feedback helps me become better."
→ "I can always improve something."
→ "Determination and perseverance will help me accomplish anything."
→ "My results don't define me."
→ "There are several ways to get from point A to point B."

Your mindset shapes a great deal of your actions and your attitude toward life. A growth mindset will help you build your problem-solving skills, curiosity, and confidence. It can also help you overcome worried thoughts because you understand you can always try again, nobody is perfect, and mistakes help you learn and grow stronger. A growth mindset also makes you better able to tackle the challenges you may face when learning something new or developing a new skill.

Next Time . . .

I received a B+ on my science quiz and felt like a failure who didn't try hard enough.

Next time, I'll remind myself that a B+ is a good grade and that I tried my best. I'll remember that no one is perfect. Also, I can learn from the mistakes I made on this quiz and do better on the next one!

GROW A GROWTH MINDSET!

Fill in the last three boxes by switching fixed-mindset thinking to growth-mindset thinking.

INSTEAD OF . . . (FIXED MINDSET)		TRY THINKING . . . (GROWTH MINDSET)
I can't do this.		I will keep trying because I *can* always improve.
I'm not good at making friends.		I'm going to smile and say hi!
I don't know how to do that.	⟷	I don't know how to do that *yet*!
This is too hard. I give up!		
It's not good enough.		
I don't understand this.		

NOBODY'S "PERFECT"

Perfectionism is the need to be, or to appear to be, perfect, or to believe it's possible to achieve perfection. It can be fueled by trying to live up to an idea you have in your head, or it might be caused by fear. Perfectionism can cause frustration, anxiety, sadness, and anger.

PERFECTIONISTIC-THINKING EXAMPLES

I NEED TO BE PERFECT, SO I MIGHT ...

... procrastinate and give up too easily.

... do something over and over to get it right.

... be overly cautious and thorough, which results in taking much longer than is needed to complete a task.

... avoid trying new things because I don't want to risk making mistakes.

It's okay to strive for excellence and to try to do your best, but it's important to understand that mistakes are going to happen. Embracing imperfection can open you up to many new experiences with less worry.

TIPS TO OVERCOME PERFECTIONISTIC THINKING

1. **Figure out if you have perfectionistic thinking.**

2. **Replace critical thoughts with more realistic thoughts daily. Remind yourself:** *Everyone makes mistakes. All I can do is my best!*

3. **Look at the big picture. Take a step back and ask yourself:** *Will the small details I am worrying about matter tomorrow? Next week?*

NOBODY'S PERFECT!

Read the following examples of kids using perfectionistic thinking. Write down what you would say to help them feel better and let them know that everything will be okay.

1. **Lily often scores high on her science tests. When she gets her recent science test back, she sees three red marks. Shocked, she thinks: *I can't believe the grade I got! I'm horrible at science.* She is very frustrated, and when she gets home, she thinks about it all night. She tells herself over and over how disappointed she is in herself.**

What could you say to Lily? _____

_____

_____

2. **Ahmed is on the swim team and often gets first place in his swim meets. But at the last few meets, he placed in second or third. He says to himself: *My parents must be so disappointed in me. I can't look at my teammates because I know how horrible they must think I am. Why did I ever think I was a good swimmer in the first place? I'm worthless. I should just quit.* He sits by himself and feels anxious and sad.**

What could you say to Ahmed? _____

_____

_____

THE GRASS IS GREENER

When we compare ourselves to others, the grass often appears greener on the other side (meaning something we don't have seems better than what we do). For example, it's easy to get wrapped up in who likes your picture on social media or how many people follow you. But people tend to post or share about only the best parts of their days and lives and will often edit their images with filters.

The same is true in school and with friends and other kids your age. You might compare who gets better grades, who is hanging out with whom, who is best at sports, etc. Comparisons can make you feel insecure and worried, so it's important to remember that what we see on the surface isn't always true. Everyone has positive and negative parts of their lives, despite what you might think. Instead of worrying about other people, it's better to focus on your own unique strengths and celebrate your own progress. Rather than comparing yourself to others, you can learn the skill of *self-comparing*. For example:

Abby enjoys running. She jogs every day and loves how good she feels after a run. She's on the track and field team at school, and after every meet, she records her time. Then she makes a goal to beat that time on her next run. To measure her progress, she compares each time to her own previous time, not to other people's. To her, it doesn't matter if someone is faster than she is. She is her own competition, and she knows that no matter what happens, she can continue to grow stronger and work toward her goal.

THE GRASS IS GREENER WHERE YOU WATER IT!

The best way to get rid of comparisons is to focus on your individual strengths, practice gratitude for what you do have, and create goals around self-competition, not competition with others. Let's practice!

IDENTIFY YOUR STRENGTHS: List three traits about yourself that are special and unique.

PRACTICE GRATITUDE: List three things, people, or personal qualities you are grateful for.

CREATE A SELF-COMPARISON GOAL

WHAT WE'VE LEARNED

In chapter 3, you learned a bunch of new and powerful ways of thinking. You learned how to notice thought traps, how to problem-solve your worries, how to overcome perfectionism and comparisons, and how to develop a growth mindset. This will help you build your confidence as you progress through the next chapters.

In this chapter, I learned:

Learning this information is helpful because:

So far, the most helpful idea or exercise for me is:

CHAPTER FOUR

Emotions and the Body

In this chapter, you will learn how worry affects your emotional and physical reactions. You will explore how your emotions are connected to worry, why you experience certain emotions, and how emotions show up in your body. You will discover how to learn from your emotions, embrace all your emotions, cope with stress, and practice gratitude.

UNDERSTANDING FEELINGS

Everyone experiences a wide range of emotions. It is normal to experience both positive emotions and challenging emotions throughout the day. However, it is important to remember that no emotion or feeling is "bad." In fact, while some emotions don't feel pleasant, they can be useful messengers that provide important information about what's going on around us. They can also tell us what we might need (emotionally) or what we need to do to improve a situation.

To understand our emotions and feelings, we first must notice and identify them. Common feelings associated with worry include anxiety, fear, and nervousness. Other feelings connected with worry are irritability, frustration, anger, and sadness. For example:

Julia is snowboarding for the first time when someone skis past her quickly, making her lose her balance and fall to the ground. Julia is furious. As she feels the anger rising in her body, she remembers it can help to identify and name the emotion she is feeling. She thinks: *I am feeling angry.* She then asks herself: *What is behind my anger?* She realizes: *It's worry hidden behind my anger. I'm feeling anxious and worried that I could get hurt because this is my first time snowboarding. My worry is making me feel a little on edge about things, and I'm quicker to anger.*

Another example:

Zane is invited to a party where he won't know anyone. Before the party, his stomach begins to hurt, and he thinks he must be sick and shouldn't go. Then he remembers that the last time he met new people, he had a stomachache, too. He thinks: *My body is sending me a sign. I'm feeling a little nervous, but once I go and have fun, the feeling will go away.*

EMOTION EXPLORER

How do you look when you feel different things? Draw in eyes, eyebrows, a nose, and a mouth to create a face that shows each emotion below. Then write when you experienced each specific emotion. Think about what thoughts or worries were connected to that emotion.

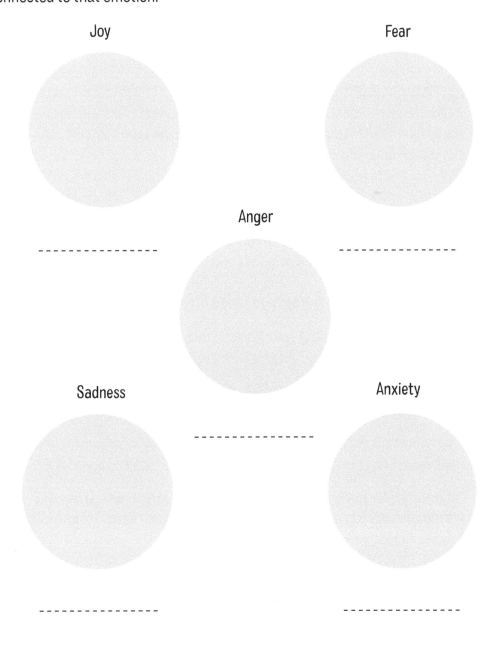

Joy

Fear

- - - - - - - - - - - - - - - -   - - - - - - - - - - - - - - - -

Anger

Sadness

Anxiety

- - - - - - - - - - - - - - - -

- - - - - - - - - - - - - - - -   - - - - - - - - - - - - - - - -

WHY DO I FEEL THIS WAY?

Once you can identify your emotions, it is also helpful to figure out what's causing them. Think of emotions as visitors that come and go. They send us important messages about what we or our bodies might be needing. Once we figure out the message, we are better able to work through uncomfortable feelings.

For example, sadness might be telling you that you need to cry. Anxiety might be telling you that you need to slow down and breathe. Loneliness might be telling you that you need connection. Emptiness might be telling you that you need to try something new. Anger might be telling you that you need to check in with your boundaries and take a break.

TIPS FOR IDENTIFYING EMOTIONS AND THEIR CAUSE

1. **What is your body telling you? If you're unsure, look in the mirror: How does your face look? Angry? Sad? Excited?**

2. **Check in with other bodily signs: Is your heart beating fast? Is your body tense? Are you crying or close to crying?**

3. **Ask yourself: *Did a situation trigger me? Did I have an argument with someone? Do I have a lot to do? Am I lonely? Am I tired or hungry?***

4. **Once you identify the emotion and its cause, ask yourself: *What is my anger, anxiety, or sadness telling me? What do I need right now in order to feel better?***

5. **Listen to what you need, and make a plan to address that need.**

NAME YOUR FEELING AND BEGIN THE HEALING

Fill in each line with the emotion you might feel in the given situation. Use the word bank or choose your own!

WORD BANK

Anxious	Happy	Relaxed
Calm	Irritable	Resentful
Content	Jealous	Sad
Embarrassed	Lonely	Stressed
Excited	Overwhelmed	Tired
Frustrated	Peaceful	Worried
Grateful	Proud	

When I am hungry, I might feel _____.

When someone encourages me, I might feel _____.

When someone leaves me out at school, I might feel _____.

When I get the answer wrong in class, I might feel _____.

When I name my strengths and positive qualities, I might feel

_____.

When I go for a walk, I might feel _____.

When I am tired, I might feel _____.

continued →

When someone points out something I am good at, I might feel

- .

When I am trying something new, I might feel - .

When I get into an argument, I might feel -

- .

When someone includes me, I might feel - .

When a friend has something that I really want, I might feel

- .

When I don't do well on a test, I might feel - .

When I exercise, I might feel - .

When I am lonely, I might feel - .

When a friend is being unkind, I might feel - .

When I forgive someone, I might feel - .

When I am holding on to a grudge, I might feel - .

When I have a lot of chores to do, I might feel - .

When I change my negative thoughts to more helpful ones, I might feel

- .

When I am kind and include others, I might feel - .

When I am going on a vacation soon, I might feel - .

When I practice yoga or meditation, I might feel - .

When I practice gratitude, I might feel - .

EMOTIONS IN THE BODY

It can be helpful to learn how your body reacts to different emotions. You might feel anxiety in your stomach, sadness in your chest, or stress in your head—the experience of emotion is different for everyone. Emotions can also show up as warmth, chills, a fast heart rate, sweating, tense shoulders, a clenched jaw, and more.

When these feelings become too intense, you might feel overwhelmed or panicked. An extreme version of this is called a *panic attack*. This is when fear and anxiety come over you suddenly. You might have shortness of breath and feel disconnected from yourself or your surroundings. This could be in response to something you feel threatened by, or it could be out of the blue, but in either case, you aren't in any real and immediate danger.

However you personally experience emotion, use those signals as a reminder to slow down and explore your thoughts and worries and as a coping strategy. No matter the emotion, it is always helpful to pause, breathe, and take a few moments to relax your body. This sends a message back to your brain that all is well, which allows your mind to relax and helps you find calm. For example:

Lin is going to a new art camp. He does not know anyone and feels his stomach start to ache. He thinks: *I am feeling anxious. I often feel a little anxiety in my stomach and get nervous when I try something new. Then, once I try it, I feel better, and my stomachache goes away. I love art, and I can do this!*

ME AND MY HAPPY PLACE

When you experience stress and challenging emotions, your body sends you signs. You might have a fast heart rate, feel tense, or have pain in your stomach. In the same way, your body lets you know when you are experiencing positive emotions and a lack of stress. You might feel relaxed, or you could be energized. You might feel focused, calm, happy, excited, grateful, or peaceful.

Draw a picture below of you when you are worry-free. What does your body look like? How do you feel? Where are you? What are you doing?

GETTING UNCOMFORTABLE

All emotions are a part of life, but some people try to push away emotions that they don't like in order to avoid pain. This doesn't make those emotions go away—they keep piling up. Burying emotions we don't want can negatively affect our brains and our bodies in the long term.

Emotions that aren't dealt with can lead to stress, anxiety, and issues connecting with others. It is important to learn how to feel your emotions—especially the hard ones.

TIPS FOR COPING WITH UNCOMFORTABLE FEELINGS

→ Take a *mindful moment* to pause and be with yourself.
→ Acknowledge the emotion, but know that it is not who you are. Remember the phrase "Name it to tame it."
→ Show self-compassion. Practice caring about your pain instead of avoiding it. Remember the phrase "Feel it to heal it."
→ Remind yourself that all emotions come and go.

Next Time . . .

I had a bad day at school, and I was feeling different emotions all at once. I didn't like how they felt, so I kept pushing them away. I felt tense and unhappy for days.

Next time, I'll remind myself that all emotions are okay to have. I'll journal about the emotions I'm feeling. I can also use mindfulness to help me feel better.

I ACCEPT MY EMOTIONS, BUT I AM NOT MY EMOTIONS

Practice these steps and answer the questions to learn how to embrace your emotions rather than push them away.

STEP 1: NAME THE EMOTION

Sit and pay attention to your thoughts and physical sensations. What emotion are you feeling? _

STEP 2: GET SPACE

Close your eyes and imagine putting that emotion five feet in front of you. You are putting this emotion outside yourself so you can take a better look at it.

STEP 3: GIVE THE EMOTION A FORM

If your emotion had a shape, what shape would it be? _

If your emotion had a size, how big would it be? _

If your emotion had a color, what color would it be? _

If your emotion had a texture, what texture would it be? _

If your emotion had a temperature, would it be cold, warm, or hot? _ _ _ _ _ _ _ _ _ _ _ _ _

Once you have given your emotion a form, close your eyes again and watch it for a few minutes. Recognize that the emotion is part of your experience at this moment, but also recognize that you are not the emotion. Now you can place the emotion back inside yourself or set it free, whatever you feel like you need in this moment.

STEP 4: REFLECTION

Reflect on what you noticed. Did you feel any change in the emotion once you gave it a name or when you got some distance from it? What about when you gave it a form? How does the emotion feel now?

_ _

_ _

UNDERSTANDING STRESS

Stress and worry are connected, but they are different. Worry happens in your mind, while stress is felt in your body. Stress can be described as your body's physical response to mental or emotional pressures, and it can affect your body in lots of ways: Stress can cause changes in your blood pressure, heart rate, and blood sugar levels. Or it might give you a stomachache, a headache, or even trouble sleeping. Too much stress is uncomfortable and can hurt your physical and emotional health.

Here is an example of how stress and worry are related:

Oliver is afraid of sleeping alone in his room at night in the dark. He has a recurring worry: *What if something bad happens and my parents can't hear me?* Around bedtime each night, his body shows signs of stress—his heart beats faster, he begins to sweat, and his stomach starts to hurt. He has difficulty sleeping, and when he does fall asleep, he sometimes has nightmares.

It's important to remember that stress is very common. If you experience stress, you are not alone. There are a lot of ways you can reduce stress. One powerful way is to practice deep-breathing exercises. Deep-breathing exercises increase the oxygen to your brain and promote calmness. They take the focus off your worries and help you get rid of tension in your body.

By being mindful and combatting negative thoughts, you can also help reduce stress.

DEEP-BREATHING TECHNIQUES TO PRACTICE

Star Breathing

Trace the star, breathing in, then out.
Repeat 3 times, or until you feel calm.

Box Breathing

Trace the square as you breathe.
Repeat 3 times, or until you feel calm.

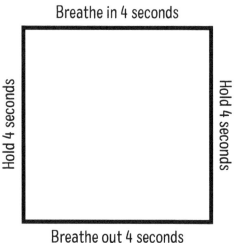

How do you feel after doing the exercise?

How do you feel after doing the exercise?

Which exercise was your favorite? Why do you think that is?

BUTTERFLY HUG

Practice the butterfly hug to calm and soothe yourself when you are feeling worried and stressed.

Before beginning, take a moment and close your eyes.

What emotion(s) do you feel? _

Imagine you are in a place that is calm, safe, and peaceful. Imagine the colors, sounds, and scents in your safe place.

What do you see? _

What do you hear? _

What do you smell? _

STEP 1: Cross your arms over your chest and place your hands on your shoulders. These are your butterfly wings.

STEP 2: Gently begin tapping on your shoulders, first with one hand, then the other, alternating sides like you are gently flapping your wings. Tap 10 times.

STEP 3: Pause and take a deep breath.

What is something kind you can say to yourself? _

STEP 4: Continue tapping your shoulders until you feel more relaxed.

What emotions are you feeling now? _

What thoughts do you have? _

How does your body feel? _

RESPONDING TO WHAT YOU FEEL

Although we can't control which emotions and physical sensations we feel during stressful moments, we *can* learn coping strategies to better address stress. People often react negatively to stress. They might feel overwhelmed and act out, yell, or shut down. But with self-reflection and the proper coping tools, you can choose how you respond to stress. Begin by reflecting on and exploring your personal stressors and reactions to stress. Stress and worry go hand in hand, so learning to recognize how you react to stress and what specifically stresses you out is key to finding the coping tools that work best for you, your mind, and your body.

STEPS FOR COPING WITH STRESS

1. **IDENTIFY YOUR STRESSORS: Start keeping track of your stress level and stressors in a daily journal. Ask yourself: *What caused my stress? Was it a certain person or situation? How was I feeling at the time? How do I act when I'm stressed?***

2. **CHANGE YOUR STRESSORS: What stressors can you change? For example, if lack of sleep is an issue, can you set an earlier bedtime or change your bedtime routine so you get more sleep?**

3. **SET LIMITS: Do you feel overwhelmed with what you have to do? Ask yourself: *Am I overloaded with activities? What activities could I limit?***

4. **PRACTICE SELF-CARE AND COPING SKILLS: Explore what works for you.**

5. **TALK TO SOMEONE: Who can you talk to that you trust?**

REDUCE STRESS WITH JOURNALING

Start your journal now! Think about the last time you felt stressed, and answer the questions below.

What happened the last time you felt stressed?

_____

_____

How did you react to the stress?

_____

_____

What do you think triggered your stress? Was it a certain person or situation?

_____

_____

What was going on in your environment? Were you tired or hungry?

_____

_____

What can you change next time to avoid the stress or handle it better or differently?

_____

_____

_____

PROGRESSIVE MUSCLE RELAXATION

Try out this simple strategy of tensing and relaxing your muscles. Once you've learned it and practiced a few times, you can use it whenever you might be feeling stressed, and you can do it anywhere! For example, if you're feeling stressed or emotional at school, you can do this right in your seat. And remember, if your stress level gets too high, reach out to your school counselor for help.

→ Take 3 deep breaths.
→ Scrunch up your forehead (as if you are thinking hard) for 5 seconds. Relax.
→ Squeeze your eyes closed for 5 seconds. Relax.
→ Shrug your shoulders for 5 seconds. Relax.
→ Tense your arm muscles for 5 seconds. Relax.
→ Tense your hand muscles for 5 seconds. Relax.
→ Tense your stomach muscles for 5 seconds. Relax.
→ Tense your leg muscles for 5 seconds. Relax.
→ Tense your foot for 5 seconds. Relax.
→ Tense all your muscles for 5 seconds. Relax.
→ Take 3 deep breaths.

Once you have completed two rounds of this stress-reducing exercise, check off any results you experienced from practicing it.

☐ Calm, slow heart rate

☐ Relaxed shoulders

☐ Relaxed legs

☐ Relaxed jaw

☐ Relaxed body

☐ Feeling focused/clear thoughts

☐ Positive thoughts

☐ Feeling peaceful and content

☐ Feeling comfortable, relaxed, and calm

☐ Feeling energized and ready for the day

LOOK TO THE SKY!

No matter where you are out in the world—on a bus, out for a nature walk, or just around your neighborhood—grounding techniques are useful strategies to combat stress. These techniques help you focus on the present moment rather than on the future or the past. Some of these techniques include breathing exercises like the ones you've practiced earlier in the book, and others allow your mind to take a moment to calm down by focusing on something else. For example, you can take a moment to look for shapes in the clouds. Take a deep breath, relax your mind, and let your imagination fly.

Step outside and look at the clouds. Can you find the following pictures in the clouds? Check them off if you find them, and add any others you see.

☐ Hippo   ☐ Car

☐ Cartoon character   ☐ _____

☐ Horse   ☐ _____

☐ Lion   ☐ _____

☐ Spaceship   ☐ _____

☐ Elephant   ☐ _____

☐ Jellyfish   ☐ _____

☐ Face   ☐ _____

LOOKING FOR THE POSITIVES

One way to bounce back from difficult emotions and stress is to refocus on the positive things and people in your life or in the world around you. When you practice gratitude daily, you develop a new pattern for your brain, which helps you make more positive thoughts and have less worry. When you express gratitude, your brain releases dopamine and serotonin, two hormones that make us feel happier. Also, gratitude can strengthen our friendships, because when we feel grateful for others and tell them so, we feel closer and more connected.

GRATITUDE CAN BE GROWN WITH A FEW SIMPLE STEPS

1. RECOGNIZE the gifts and people in your life. Shift your focus from what isn't working and what you don't have in your life to what is working and the things and people you do have.

2. ACKNOWLEDGE what you are grateful for and the positive role others play in your life.

3. EXPRESS your appreciation for something or someone by telling them about it. (For example, write a letter to a friend, a family member, a teacher, or someone you trust and admire to let them know how you feel.)

MY DAILY GRATITUDE CALENDAR

When you practice gratitude daily, you develop positive thoughts and a positive mindset! Keep a journal and write down what you are thankful for each day.

For each day of the week, fill in three things or people you are thankful for, and why.

SUNDAY	I am thankful for → → → Because I can show my gratitude by
MONDAY	I am thankful for → → → Because I can show my gratitude by
TUESDAY	I am thankful for → → → Because I can show my gratitude by

continued →

WEDNESDAY	I am thankful for → → → Because I can show my gratitude by
THURSDAY	I am thankful for → → → Because I can show my gratitude by
FRIDAY	I am thankful for → → → Because I can show my gratitude by
SATURDAY	I am thankful for → → → Because I can show my gratitude by

WHAT WE'VE LEARNED

In chapter 4, you learned a variety of new ways to understand and handle your emotions. You explored how worry affects your emotions, why you have certain emotions, and how your body responds to emotions. You also learned different ways you can accept all your emotions (even the uncomfortable ones), cope with stress, and show gratitude. All this will help you better manage your worries and prepare you for the next chapters.

In this chapter, I learned:

Learning this information is helpful because:

So far, the most helpful idea or exercise for me is:

CHAPTER FIVE

Facing Your Fears

In this chapter, you will learn how to face your fears and how to recognize and let go of avoidance and safety behaviors. You will learn how to define your fears, take small steps toward challenging them, and explore and practice different ways to build confidence and bravery.

BEING BRAVE

The first step in facing your fear is to name it. After you name your fear, it's important to evaluate the likelihood of that fear coming true. You can do this by looking at the worst-case, best-case, and most likely possibilities. You will usually find that the worst-case possibility is not very likely to happen.

Speaking in front of a class, participating in new activities, and meeting new people are common fears. For example:

Zheng recently moved to town and wanted to meet new friends, but he was afraid that his new classmates wouldn't like him. He was very quiet and rarely talked to anyone at school or on the bus. One day on the bus, he decided to face his fear and say hi to Weston. Weston said hi back. The next day, Zheng asked Weston if he could sit with him on the bus, and Weston said yes. They began talking about video games and soon became good friends. Zheng realized that the worst-case possibility did not happen. He was glad that he had faced his fear.

It's important to practice putting yourself in different situations, even when you are a bit uncomfortable. When you face your fears, you challenge your worries and can learn not to listen to them. Even if you feel a little worried, you can remind yourself which possibility is the most likely to happen. With each step, you learn that you can do hard things and work toward overcoming your fears.

IDENTIFY FEARS

What is one of your biggest fears?

What is the worst-case scenario for that fear?

On a scale of 1 to 10, what is the likelihood of the worst-case scenario coming true?

← 1 — 2 — 3 — 4 — 5 — 6 — 7 — 8 — 9 — 10 →

Not Likely   Very Likely

What is the best-case scenario for that fear?

On a scale of 1 to 10, what is the likelihood of the best-case scenario coming true?

← 1 — 2 — 3 — 4 — 5 — 6 — 7 — 8 — 9 — 10 →

Not Likely   Very Likely

What is the most likely scenario for that fear?

← 1 — 2 — 3 — 4 — 5 — 6 — 7 — 8 — 9 — 10 →

Not Likely   Very Likely

STEP-BY-STEP

When facing your fears and worries, it's important to take small, slow steps toward overcoming them. Smaller steps are less overwhelming, and they make facing your fears more manageable and comfortable. You can plan to take your first step by creating a goal, beginning with a situation that causes you the least worry and stress, then working your way up.

A great way to plan this out is to create a "Bravery Ladder." First you need to identify your fear and create a goal. This goal is the top rung of the ladder because it will be your last step. Then create smaller goals leading up to that top rung—overcoming your fear. Begin with a small goal that causes you the least amount of fear and work your way up the ladder. For example:

Simon has a fear of public speaking and has to give a presentation in class soon. He learned about the Bravery Ladder from his school counselor and decided to start facing his fear by practicing his presentation in the mirror. After practicing in the mirror, he moved up the ladder to practicing in front of his dog, Max. When he felt ready, he practiced in front of his parents. Soon he was ready for his presentation in front of his class!

Just like Simon, as you climb each step and expose yourself to your fear little by little, you will become more comfortable and confident.

THE BRAVERY LADDER

Finish Tierra's Bravery Ladder, and then create your own!

TIERRA'S FEAR: Tierra is afraid of talking to people she doesn't know.
TIERRA'S GOAL: To feel confident enough to make new friends.

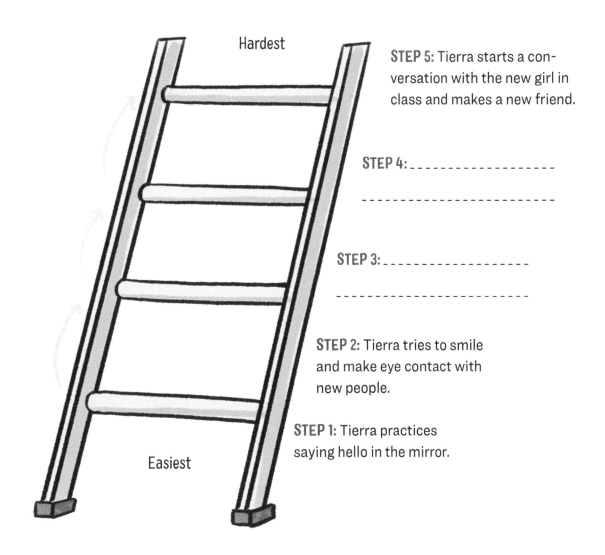

Hardest

STEP 5: Tierra starts a conversation with the new girl in class and makes a new friend.

STEP 4: _____

_____

STEP 3: _____

_____

STEP 2: Tierra tries to smile and make eye contact with new people.

STEP 1: Tierra practices saying hello in the mirror.

Easiest

continued →

MY BRAVERY LADDER

MY FEAR: ---

MY GOAL: ---

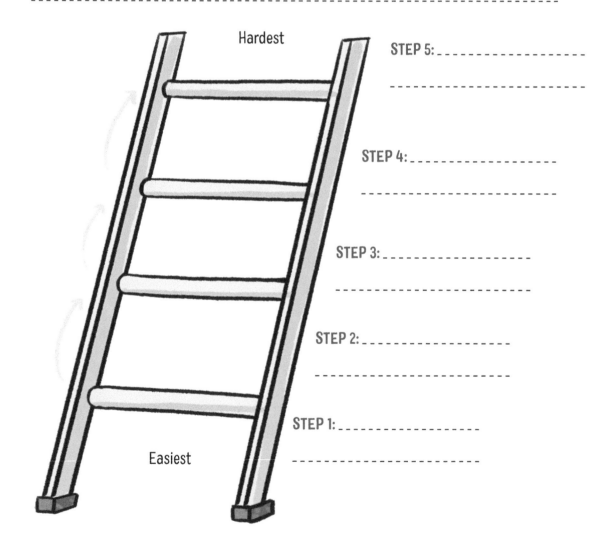

Hardest

STEP 5: -------------------

STEP 4: -------------------

STEP 3: -------------------

STEP 2: -------------------

STEP 1: -------------------

Easiest

AVOIDANCE BEHAVIORS

A behavior is how someone acts. It can be what a person does to make something happen, to make something change, or just to keep things the same. Avoidance behaviors are actions people use to escape difficult thoughts, feelings, or situations. As you know, anxiety can cause a fight-flight-freeze response in the brain. Avoidance behaviors are the flight response in situations that are not actually dangerous.

Some examples of avoidance behaviors are pretending you are sick to avoid a presentation or test, canceling plans at the last minute, procrastinating, and not answering calls or texts.

When you try to push away stress instead of letting yourself feel your emotions, you give yourself a false sense of control. You might feel better in the moment, but you're actually giving control to your worry. Avoiding situations not only makes worries and anxiety stronger, it also makes you less likely to explore the world, take chances, and discover activities you might love. To change avoidance behaviors, think about what avoidance behaviors you have and face them little by little.

TIPS FOR FACING AVOIDANCE BEHAVIORS

1. **Write down your avoidance behaviors. Do you often give excuses for things you don't want to do?**

2. **Write down the fear behind your avoidance behaviors.**

3. **Remind yourself of the times the feared situation hasn't happened, or happened but wasn't as bad as you expected.**

4. **Slowly expose yourself to your fear in small, gradual steps.**

5. **Share your fear with a trusted adult or by journaling.**

FEAR NOT!

1. **What is one avoidance behavior you use?**

   ----

2. **What is the fear behind this avoidance behavior?**

   ----

3. **Write down a time when you didn't avoid the feared situation, and everything turned out okay.**

   ----

4. **Write down one step you could take to change this unhelpful behavior and one benefit of changing this avoidance behavior.**

   ----

5. **Share your fears, and your plans to address your avoidance behaviors and challenge your fears, with a trusted adult and/or in your journal.**

SAFETY-SEEKING BEHAVIORS

Many people with anxiety use *safety-seeking behaviors* to protect themselves. Safety-seeking behaviors are actions that people think will help prevent a specific situation from happening. Some safety-seeking behaviors can be helpful. For example, looking both ways before crossing a road or checking the temperature of shower water before getting in.

Examples of unhelpful safety-seeking behaviors include overplanning, staying close to home, and keeping the lights on at night. When safety-seeking behaviors are in response to perceived threats rather than actual dangers, they can worsen or increase your anxiety. They can also prevent you from trying new or different activities. To change these worried thoughts and unhelpful safety-seeking behaviors in the long run and reduce your anxiety, you must learn to recognize them.

TIPS FOR RECOGNIZING AND CHANGING UNHELPFUL BEHAVIORS

1. **Look for behaviors that feel urgent and aimed at reducing stress. Write these down and decide if they are helpful or unhelpful.**

2. **Practice resisting the unhelpful behaviors. When you feel the urge to use a safety-seeking behavior, pause and remind yourself that each time you tolerate a little anxiety, it gets easier to do so.**

3. **Replace these behaviors with more useful behaviors. For example, if you keep the lights on all night, plan to try something else to calm you, like listening to your favorite song before bed.**

TRANSFORMING ANXIETY

What safety-seeking behaviors can you think of? Are they helpful or unhelpful? Can you change your unhelpful behaviors to helpful ones to transform your anxiety? Fill in the table below to help you examine your own behaviors. There's an example to get you started.

BEHAVIOR	HELPFUL OR UNHELPFUL?	HOW TO CHANGE IF UNHELPFUL
Constantly checking social media	Unhelpful	Turn phone off while you go for a walk

WHEN THINGS GET HARD

In her book *Resilience*, author and inspirational speaker Elizabeth Edwards wrote, "She stood in the storm, and when the wind did not blow her way—and it surely has not—she adjusted her sails." This means that we can't control the situations and experiences that life presents us with, but we can control how we respond to them. We can find healthy and productive ways to move forward when things change or don't go our way.

Hard things happen to all of us, and if we try to control them or resist change, we get stuck. But when we "adjust our sails," or find ways to adapt to difficult situations, we can brave the storm—and come out stronger.

When you overcome hard things, you develop the confidence that you will be able to do so again in the future. As you discover your inner strengths, you build self-confidence and the ability to bounce back from tough times.

WHAT TO DO WHEN THINGS GET HARD

1. **Identify the challenge: What feels too hard or overwhelming for you?**

2. **Acknowledge your emotions and name the feelings you are experiencing.**

3. **Think about hard times you have experienced in the past and how you overcame them successfully.**

4. **Imagine yourself overcoming this new challenge. Think about the steps you can take to get you there.**

5. **Repeat positive affirmations and mindful mantras to encourage and motivate you.**

6. **Journal each time you come across something difficult and overcome the challenge.**

MY EMOTIONS ARE LIKE CLOUDS

At home, you might worry about things like homework and getting along with your family members. This can lead to uncomfortable feelings. It's important to remember that emotions come and go like clouds. Sometimes they are dark, stormy, and heavy. Other times they are white and fluffy. They are always moving and changing. When we experience challenging emotions and worries, it's helpful to have a plan with some ideas of different ways we could feel better. This exercise will help you make a plan for how to manage your emotions on difficult days.

Identify four different emotions and write each in a cloud, then fill in what you can do if you experience those emotions.

If I feel . . .

I can _

_ _

_ .

If I feel . . .

I can _

_ _

_ .

If I feel . . .

I can _

_ _

_ .

If I feel . . .

I can _

_ _

_ .

SAYING IS BELIEVING

The more positive things you say about yourself, the more you believe them! The same goes for negative self-talk. Have you ever felt that you're not any good at a particular subject in school just because it takes you a little longer to learn it? That's why it's so important to make positive statements about yourself—it boosts your self-confidence!

Repeat these five positive affirmations for getting through hard times, then write down five of your own. Write them somewhere you can read them easily throughout the school day so they can encourage you when you have worried thoughts.

1.   **I can learn anything with effort and practice.**

2.   **I believe in my abilities.**

3.   **I am stronger than my fears.**

4.   **I can do hard things.**

5.   **I am grateful for everything I've accomplished so far.**

YOU TRY!

1.   -

2.   -

3.   -

4.   -

5.   -

POSITIVE VIBES HELP ME THRIVE!

Many things happen out in the world that we can't control, but we *can* control how we react to them. Mantras are helpful ways to combat those world worries when they do hit. Mantras are positive words or phrases that are great motivators to say over and over when you're struggling. When you chant mantras, your mind releases positive energy, which lowers your stress. Practice your mindful mantras anywhere out in the world, and you will feel more empowered to face any worries!

Recite these five confidence-boosting mindful mantras for getting through hard times, then write five of your own.

1. **Positive vibes help me thrive!**

2. **I create my own path and walk it with joy.**

3. **I do my best and forget the rest.**

4. **No pressure, no diamonds!**

5. **Challenges help me grow stronger.**

YOU TRY!

1. _____

2. _____

3. _____

4. _____

5. _____

TALK ABOUT IT

I t is important to practice talking about how you are feeling. Communication is a valuable skill to have in life. It is also important, though, to find people in our lives who we can communicate with openly and honestly. Talking through your emotions and worried thoughts is a healthy coping strategy.

It helps to identify a trusted adult who you can talk to about your thoughts, feelings, problems, and needs. A trusted adult is an adult you feel safe with, someone you can be yourself around and who wants the best for you. Your person could be a parent, a school counselor or teacher, or any other trusted adult in your life.

Friends can offer support and encouragement, too, and while it's good to have trusted friends you can confide in, it's very important to find at least one adult you can talk to about your worries. This is because the rational part of the brain isn't fully developed until age 25, so trusted adults are an essential part of your mental health and wellness.

TIPS FOR OPENING UP

1. **Identify the worried thoughts, feelings, and problems you'd like to overcome and write them down.**

2. **Write down the names of three trusted adults you can reach out to when you need to.**

3. **Think about ways you could express how you're feeling to the trusted adults you identified. Do you want to write them a letter, send them a text, or ask them if they can talk with you one-on-one?**

WHO CAN I TALK TO?

Name three adults who you trust and feel comfortable talking to.

1. -

2. -

3. -

Circle your favorite way to reach out to a trusted adult.

Write a letter

Send an email   Text

Video chat   Phone call

Talk in person

What would you write or say to them?

- -

- -

- -

THE KEYS TO CONFIDENCE

Self-confidence is when you believe in or trust your abilities, qualities, and judgment. If you struggle with self-confidence, you are not alone. Lots of people struggle with confidence, especially in their preteen years.

When you build self-confidence, you are getting ready for life's experiences. You are more likely to try new things and not be afraid to be yourself. You don't have to fake anything or prove yourself to anyone. You are kind to others and don't feel intimidated by their strengths. You understand that everyone has unique strengths, abilities, and talents, including you. You understand how to stand up for yourself and others when necessary. You have a growth mindset, and you know that everyone makes mistakes and everyone encounters both failures and successes. You can take healthy risks and are not afraid of failure. You know you can try again and that, with effort and practice, you will become stronger and more capable.

Rather than shying away from something new, confidence helps you move forward, and if things don't work out at first, self-confidence and resilience will motivate you to try again.

continued →

The Keys to Confidence, *continued*

HOW TO BUILD SELF-CONFIDENCE

1. Think of the things you're good at: your strengths, passions, and abilities.

2. Look back on your past accomplishments. Write them down. Draw them.

3. Create goals around your strengths and passions to grow in these areas. For example: Do you love art? Try an art class. Do you love animals? Volunteer at an animal shelter or start a dog-walking business in your neighborhood.

4. Recite positive affirmations and mindful mantras daily.

5. Explore a new hobby or friendship.

Next Time . . .

My friend told me they didn't want to be friends with me anymore. I have been so upset that I told my parents I was sick and couldn't go to school.

Next time, I will *go to school. I'll use positive affirmations to help me. I'll think:* I am valuable. I am a good friend. I will make new friends who appreciate me. *I'll reach out to a parent or the school counselor to talk about it.*

I HAVE CONFIDENCE!

Read through the example, then write a situation where you showed self-confidence or in which you'd like to show self-confidence in the future. Describe your thoughts, feelings, and actions, and practice unlocking the door to self-confidence!

Example:

SITUATION OR EVENT: I am attending a party where I don't know many people.

CONFIDENT THOUGHTS:	CONFIDENT FEELINGS:	CONFIDENT ACTIONS:
I am a good communicator. Making new friends is fun!	Nervous, but excited.	At the party, I will introduce myself. Smile. I will not judge myself. I will have fun!

YOUR TURN!

SITUATION OR EVENT:

CONFIDENT THOUGHTS:	CONFIDENT FEELINGS:	CONFIDENT ACTIONS:

DEAR MAGNIFICENT ME!

Write a letter to yourself that you can read when you are not feeling confident.

Dear Me,

My favorite thing about myself is _____.

I am good at _____.

One of my accomplishments is _____.

A compliment I have received is _____.

I love it when I _____.

I am a good friend because _____.

Some of my hobbies and interests are _____.

I want to be more _____ with myself.

I am worthy of _____.

I am _____.

Love,

_____

WHAT WE'VE LEARNED

In chapter 5, you learned how to face your worries and fears and how to recognize, confront, and conquer avoidance and safety-seeking behaviors. You also learned how important it is to name your fears. And you practiced taking the necessary steps toward overcoming those fears, which leads to the development of self-assurance and bravery.

All of these are useful strategies that will boost your self-confidence and help you feel prepared for all that life brings your way!

In this chapter, I learned:

- -

- -

- -

Learning this information is helpful because:

- -

- -

- -

So far, the most helpful idea or exercise for me is:

- -

- -

CHAPTER SIX

Putting It into Practice

In this chapter, you will learn how to take a hands-on approach to your worry by practicing more healthy habits. You will also learn how to handle feelings of self-doubt in social situations. You will explore the effects of too much screen time and learn how to better balance the use of your devices. You will also learn about noticing and rewarding your progress, and even how to reshape your brain to be more positive and powerful.

TACKLING WORRY

Everyone's worries are a little bit different, but there are some common things that many people worry about. People commonly worry about situations involving their family, their friends, their safety, and how they are perceived by others.

No matter what challenges your day brings, it's easier to face the world when your stress is low. The best way to reduce your stress and worries is to take a hands-on approach to your mental health. That way, when you do encounter a stressful situation, you are ready to face it calmly, because you have already taken practical steps to keep your stress low and your mood elevated.

But how can you prepare when you don't know what stressful situations you might encounter? The secret lies in these three areas—physical activity, sleep, and healthy food. Take a moment and think about your daily level of physical activity, reflect on how much sleep you are getting each night, and think about what types of foods you are eating.

THREE WAYS TO TAKE ACTION AGAINST WORRY

1. **Aim for 9 to 12 hours of sleep each night to function at your best.**

2. **Strive for one or more hours of moderate to strong physical activity daily.**

3. **Eat mood-boosting foods and well-balanced meals that include plenty of whole foods, including vegetables, fruits, whole grains, nuts, and legumes. Avoid foods with labels that list lots of ingredients you cannot pronounce.**

RUN YOUR WORRIES AWAY

Did you know that one of the quickest ways to reduce stress and anxiety is to exercise?

There are many ways to be physically active. You could go for a walk or a jog, ride your bike, or play tag. It's important to explore what types of exercises work best for you and your body. The key is to find ways to be physically active that you find fun and enjoyable, because that will make you more likely to actually do those activities.

Circle at least three forms of physical activity, or fill in an activity you do or would like to try.

Baseball	Jog	Ski
Basketball	Jump rope	Soccer
Bike	Jumping jacks	Stretch
Dance	Martial arts	Swim
Football	Rollerblade	Tag
Gymnastics	Row	Tennis
Hike	Run	Walk
Ice-skate	Skateboard	Yoga

Other: _____

EAT, SLEEP, AND BE MERRY!

When you nourish your body with rest, physical activity, and well-balanced meals of healthy foods, you set the stage for a strong mind and body, which helps protect you from stress.

Remember, kids your age need between 9 and 12 hours of sleep each night. And a well-balanced diet means one full of fruits and vegetables and other healthy choices. Tip: The more colorful your plate is (think lots of fruits and veggies), the better!

Understanding the connection between your habits and your mental health can help you problem-solve and ultimately make better choices for yourself, your body, and your mind. Although you cannot completely prevent stress and anxiety from happening, you can look around to see what changes you can make to help reduce and avoid worried feelings.

Think about your healthy habits as you answer the questions below.

How many hours of sleep do you typically get per night? _

If necessary, how can you plan to get more sleep each night? (For example, could you reduce screen time or do something relaxing to unwind before bed?)

_ _

What types of foods do you usually eat each day?

_ _

If necessary, how can you plan to have more well-balanced and colorful meals?

_ _

The next time you are stressed, ask yourself: *Have I been sleeping enough? Did I go to bed at a good time? How have I been eating? Have I been getting enough physical activity? What else is going on in my environment that could be influencing my mood?*

SAFETY

Concern about safety is often a cause of worry. Some common safety worries kids have include the possibility that they or their loved ones will get injured or sick, being around strangers, and being bullied. It's normal to want to protect yourself from danger. For our early human ancestors, worrying served this purpose; if they worried about a potential threat, they were more prepared for it.

However, even though the world today is much safer in many ways, we often still respond to a feeling of danger or an unsafe situation by experiencing the fight-flight-freeze response. Think about a difficult situation, the kind that requires prompt action. You could face it head-on (fight), or you could try to leave and escape it (flight), or you could simply freeze. Have you ever felt like this? In a truly dangerous situation, the fight-flight-freeze response is useful and necessary. But the response is often triggered in situations where there is *no* true threat, and that can make you feel uneasy or unsafe for no good reason.

The next time you notice yourself feeling the urge to fight-flight-freeze, you can use the signal to challenge the worry. Ask yourself: *Am I really in an unsafe situation? Is there truly a risk? How can I switch off this response and feel safer and calmer?*

FEEL SAFE IN 1-2-3!

There are many ways we can feel safe—certain people, places, things, and beliefs can help us feel safe. It's different for everyone, so it's helpful to think about what makes you feel safe. You can work to switch off the fight-flight-freeze response when you're not really in a dangerous situation by practicing the following and filling in the questions. Then write down what makes you feel safe on the next page.

1. **KNOW THAT YOU ARE SAFE. Remind yourself that this is the fight-flight-freeze response happening right now. Think:** *This uncomfortable feeling that is making me feel unsafe is my body preparing me to run or fight. I am not in danger right now. I am okay.* **What else could you say to reassure yourself?**

   ----

2. **EXERCISE is the fastest way to manage the stress response. Just 5 to 10 minutes of movement will help break down stress hormones and signal the brain that the fight-flight-freeze response has done its job. Exercise also releases feel-good hormones called endorphins. What exercise can you do when you're stressed?**

   ----

3. **TRY TO RELAX. Practice the various exercises you have learned in this workbook, such as deep breathing, progressive muscle relaxation, the butterfly hug, or grounding techniques. Which relaxation strategy can you try?**

MY SAFE SPOTS

Three people who make me feel safe:

1. _____

2. _____

3. _____

Three exercises from this book that make me feel safe:

1. _____

2. _____

3. _____

An affirmation that makes me feel safe: _____

A place that makes me feel safe: _____

An object that makes me feel safe: _____

A belief that makes me feel safe: _____

Some other things that make me feel safe: _____

_____

SOCIAL SITUATIONS

Many people worry about social situations that might make them feel uncomfortable, such as meeting new people, speaking in front of a group, or even eating lunch with friends. This worry is called *social anxiety*, and it is quite common. For people with social anxiety, everyday social interactions can cause anxiety, fear, self-consciousness, and embarrassment. They might have an intense fear of talking with strangers or worry too much about embarrassing themselves. Social anxiety can be mild, moderate, or severe. Luckily, there are many tips and tricks to help people overcome social anxiety and manage their worries about social situations.

TIPS FOR MANAGING AND OVERCOMING SOCIAL ANXIETY

1. **Practice putting yourself in uncomfortable situations little by little, perhaps with a trusted friend or adult at first.**

2. **Keep a daily journal where you can write about your thoughts, feelings, and experiences, so that you can record and track your improvement.**

3. **Set goals around social worries. Review the Bravery Ladder on page 95 to see how you can effectively create goals to overcome your worries and anxiety step-by-step.**

4. **Improve your physical health. Exercise breaks down stress hormones and helps people manage anxiety.**

5. **Ask for help. Talk to a trusted friend, parent, or school counselor. If your social anxiety is moderate to severe, seeking help from a therapist outside school is beneficial.**

ROLE-PLAY

Role-playing social situations ahead of time with a parent, older sibling, counselor, or friend can help you feel more prepared for real-life situations. This helps you feel less anxious and more confident. Try out the sample below after you've filled in the blanks to finish the script.

THE SITUATION: You are worried about meeting a new neighbor who is around your age. You are worried that you won't know what to say or how to act around them, and that they might not like you. However, you set a goal to meet and have a conversation with your new neighbor.

You: "[*smile, wave, and give good eye contact*] Hi! My name is _ _ _ _ _ _ _ _ _ _ _ _ _ _ _ _ .

Welcome to the neighborhood!"

New Neighbor: "Hi, my name is _ ."

You: "There are a lot of kids our age to hang out with. You'll love living here!"

New Neighbor: "Thank you, I feel a little nervous being new, but I'm so happy to meet

some kids around my age."

You: "[*smiles and nods*] Do you want to _ ?"

New Neighbor: "Sure, let's go ask our parents."

(Parents say yes.)

You: "I'll introduce you to _ .

I bet they'll want to join us!"

New Neighbor: "Thanks, I'm so glad we met. I can tell we're going to be good friends."

THE NEW SITUATION: You felt anxious about meeting your new neighbor, but you faced your fear and overcame your worry. By making the goal of putting yourself out there even though you felt a little nervous, you lessened your anxiety and paved the way for it to be easier next time around. And you made a new friend!

SOCIAL ANXIETY IN SCHOOL

Make a list of five things that cause you social anxiety and stress at school.

1. _____

2. _____

3. _____

4. _____

5. _____

Create a goal for handling one of those things.

Goal: I want to reduce my social anxiety from _____

by _____

_____

_____.

SUPERHERO STANCE

Believe it or not, simply doing the Superhero Stance can reduce social anxiety and boost your confidence when you're out and about in the world! Your body is closely connected to your emotions. Even if your confidence is low, you can adjust how you feel in an instant just by changing your posture, moving forward, and smiling. Try it below and record how you feel.

HOW TO DO THE SUPERHERO STANCE

1. **Start with your feet shoulder-width apart.**

2. **Place your hands on your hips.**

3. **Hold your head up high with your chin out.**

What is one confident thought you could think? _____

4. **Push out your chest and take one step forward (as if you're preparing to move forward to conquer your stress). Circle one of the following to say out loud:**

   I am strong!

   I am brave!

   I am courageous!

   I am powerful!

   I can conquer anything!

5. **Smile, then hold this pose for 2 minutes, taking deep breaths the whole time.**

How does the Superhero Stance make you feel?

FACING REJECTION

Rejection happens when someone refuses to accept, believe, or support you. It is a common source of worry, because people have the need to belong. You might worry that someone doesn't want to be your friend or hang out with you, or that they might reject your point of view. Rejection could make you question your *self-worth*, which is the opinion you have of yourself. Having low self-worth can lead to feelings of insecurity and self-doubt. *Self-doubt* is a lack of confidence in yourself and your abilities.

Thankfully, you can learn not to fear rejection by changing your mindset! Building your self-worth is a journey. Here are some great ways to learn to value your own opinion of yourself over the opinions of others:

1.   **Write a list of your strengths.**

2.   **Remind yourself that your value is tied to your character, not your achievements.**

3.   **Recite positive affirmations and mantras, such as: "I am valuable," "I am a good friend," and "I can handle hard things!"**

4.   **If you are feeling rejected, explore other options. For example, if you didn't make the team, you can join a different club or pick up a new hobby. If you are feeling rejected by a friend, try making a new friend.**

5.   **Remember, you can always turn to a trusted adult if you are feeling rejected. Everyone experiences rejection and disagreements from time to time. You do not need to prove yourself to anyone. You are valuable and awesome just the way you are!**

BRUSH IT OFF!

Read the example, then practice how you'd respond to rejection below.

SITUATION: Two of your friends turn to you and say, "We want to play (or be) alone."

POSSIBLE THOUGHTS/RESPONSES:

→ Do not keep thinking about the rejection; instead, try to find someone else to play with.
→ Tell yourself that it's okay. Remind yourself of your many strengths.
→ Share your experience with a trusted adult if you'd like to talk about it and if you continue to experience rejection.

YOUR TURN!

SITUATION: You find out you weren't invited to someone's birthday party.

POSSIBLE THOUGHTS/RESPONSES:

1. _____
2. _____
3. _____

PRACTICE EMPATHY!

Now that you understand rejection and how it can make others feel, what are three ways you can be more accepting of others so they don't experience rejection?

1. _____
2. _____
3. _____

SCREEN TIME

Screen time is part of our lives and, in moderation, has its benefits. But spending too much time on the computer, in front of the TV, and looking at your phone can be bad for your health. Why?

PEOPLE SKILLS: More screen time can mean less time talking face-to-face with others. Face-to-face communication is essential for learning social, emotional, and life skills needed to form healthy friendships.

INACTIVE LIFESTYLE: More screen time can mean less physical activity. Physical activity helps with anxiety and worries.

FEAR OF NOT MEASURING UP: Screen time exposes you to tons of unrealistic and overedited images. Many kids compare themselves to the "life" they see in these images and feel they don't measure up.

SLEEP: Screen time right before bed can hurt both sleep quality and quantity. Good sleep helps get rid of worries and stress.

ADDICTIVE: Screen time can encourage addictive behavior. Some apps and games are designed to trigger a reward cycle in your brain. You crave the next reward, comment, or like and need another dose quickly.

Next Time . . .

I played on my iPad all day Sunday and couldn't fall asleep Sunday night. I slept in a little, barely ate any breakfast, and almost missed the bus. I felt anxious and irritable all day!

Next time, I'll remember to balance screen time with physical activity. I'll go outside with my friends or on a hike with my family.

A BALANCING ACT

How much do you know about screen time? Decide whether the statements below are true or false, and circle your answers!

1. **You cannot get addicted to screens.**   TRUE   FALSE

2. **There can be some benefits to screen time, in moderation.**   TRUE   FALSE

3. **Limiting screen time can reduce anxiety and worry.**   TRUE   FALSE

4. **Face-to-face interaction is essential for learning social, emotional, and life skills needed to form healthy relationships.**   TRUE   FALSE

5. **Too much screen time is not associated with low self-esteem.**   TRUE   FALSE

6. **If overused, screen time can affect your sleep quality and quantity.**
TRUE   FALSE

7. **Screens expose you to unrealistic and overedited images.**   TRUE   FALSE

8. **Your mental health is not affected by comparing yourself to others on screens.**
TRUE   FALSE

9. **It's important to balance screen time with physical activity.**   TRUE   FALSE

CHALLENGE YOURSELF! Try to go without screen time for two full days. Do you think you can do it? Why or why not? After two days are over, what did you notice? How did you feel? Why do you think you felt that way?

----

1. False; 2. True; 3. True; 4. True; 5. False; 6. True; 7. True; 8. False; 9. True.

REWARD YOURSELF AND HAVE FUN

You are doing an amazing job working through your worries! You should be very proud of yourself for getting to this point in the workbook. It's important to remember that when you face your fears and confront your worries, you deserve praise. It's essential to acknowledge each step, no matter how small it is.

Try it! Go ahead and congratulate yourself for getting this far! Say, "Nice work, _____." or "I am doing awesome!" or "I rock!" or whatever phrase you like. You deserve it! Complimenting yourself for your hard work and the progress you are making is important and can be very encouraging and motivating.

Have you ever given yourself rewards for creating a goal, working toward it, and achieving it? It's a fantastic strategy that can keep you motivated. Talk to your parents and friends to see if they can help support you in setting a goal and staying on track. It's great to create a goal or two around some of your worries and then reward yourself each time you try something new and step out of your comfort zone.

What is extra motivating for you? You can develop small rewards for small goals and big rewards for big goals. Each time you take a step toward working through your worries, like writing in your journal, exercising, or rewriting negative thoughts, you can reward yourself.

The benefit of learning how to manage your worries is that you have more fun and enjoy your life, and that is always the biggest reward. Always remember that you are amazing and one-of-a-kind and that you have many gifts to share with the world!

TREAT YOURSELF

When you put your mind to it, you can achieve anything! And as you create goals and take steps toward them, you should congratulate and reward yourself along the way.

1. **Name a worry that you'd like to get rid of.**

    ----

2. **Imagine yourself winning the battle over your worry.**

3. **What goal can you set connected to this worry? What steps will you take to reach that goal?**

    ----

4. **List three small rewards you could use to motivate yourself for each step.**

    ----

5. **What large reward will you get when you reach your goal?**

    ----

6. **What positive words will you say to motivate yourself as you work toward your goal?**

HAPPY BRAIN, HAPPY LIFE!

It's incredible that you can reshape your brain and train it to respond more positively when you are stressed. How cool! The brain has a quality called *neuroplasticity* that makes it possible for repeated experiences to shape the brain and even reverse the effects of stress. Like a muscle, the brain changes and gets stronger when you use it in positive ways. When you challenge your negative thoughts and create new ones, you are reshaping your brain. When you practice gratitude, positive affirmations, deep breathing, and mindfulness exercises, the same thing happens!

Throughout this workbook, you discovered useful strategies to help identify and work through your worries and emotions. You can challenge your worries by trying, practicing, and persevering. Using these strategies helps your brain grow and releases dopamine, serotonin, oxytocin, and endorphins, feel-good chemicals that help you feel better. The choices we make and how we decide to spend our time play a role in the release of those "happy chemicals." Different happy chemicals are released during the many activities and exercises you learned throughout this empowering workbook.

You now know that with dedication and practice, you can learn new ways to overcome your worrisome thoughts, and you can grow a stronger and healthier brain. You also learned that you have the power to transform your worries and develop inner confidence and a positive mindset. Keep practicing—you're doing great!

MY STRESS-LESS DAY

Plan out your stress-less day by filling in the blanks below!

1. **To have fun, I will** _____

   _____

2. **The healthy foods I will eat are** _____

   _____

3. **I will stay hydrated by** _____

   _____

4. **The types of exercise I will do are** _____

   _____

5. **If I have worried thoughts, a strategy I will use is** (Tip: Look back through the book to find your favorite strategies.) _____

   _____

   _____

6. **Another strategy I can use is** _____

   _____

7. **Another strategy I can use is** _____

   _____

8. **The positive affirmations I will say are** _____

   _____

continued →

9.   I will remember my strengths and the things I am good at, like _ _ _ _ _ _ _ _ _ _ _ _ _ _

     _ .

10. I will be kind to myself by _

     _ .

11. I will be kind to others by _

     _ .

12. If I need to talk to someone, I will talk to _

     _ .

13. To relax and wind down, I will _

     _ .

14. To get enough sleep, I will go to bed at _

     _ .

15. Before bed, I will name the things I am grateful for, such as _ _ _ _ _ _ _ _ _ _ _ _ _ _ _ _ _ _

     _ .

WHAT WE'VE LEARNED

In chapter 6, you learned how to handle social situations, screen time, feeling unsafe, and rejection. You explored how your physical health and mental health are connected and the benefits of taking action for your health. You even learned that overcoming your worries leads to a more enjoyable life!

In this chapter, I learned:

Learning this information is helpful because:

In this chapter, the most helpful idea or exercise for me is:

WEBSITES AND APPLICATIONS

GoNoodle.com
   GoNoodle provides videos, yoga activities, and mindfulness exercises for kids.

Hopscotch
joinhopscotch.com/hopscotch-family
   Hopscotch is an online platform that offers services and resources for families
   and mental health professionals, including activities kids can do at home.

Insight Timer
insighttimer.com/meditation-topics/kids-meditation
   This app has free guided meditations, including some that are just for kids.

Mindful Powers
mindfulpowersforkids.com
   Mindful Powers is an app with progressive voice-guided stories to help you relax,
   manage anxiety, and practice mindfulness.

BOOKS

Anxiety Relief Book for Kids: Activities to Understand and Overcome Worry, Fear, and Stress by Ehrin Weiss, PhD

> This book includes information and exercises that help kids build skills for finding peace and facing their fears with confidence.

The Daily Feelings Journal for Kids: A Year of Prompts to Help Kids Recognize Emotions and Express Feelings by Nathan Greene, PsyD

> This mindfulness journal is a guide to help children get comfortable with their emotions, with daily entries for tracking their feelings and weekly prompts that encourage them to dive deeper into specific feelings.

How Do I Feel? by Becca Heiden, PhD

> This guided journal helps kids learn all about emotions and how to navigate them, and the importance of caring for your mental health.

Mindfulness Workbook for Kids: 60+ Activities to Focus, Stay Calm, and Make Good Choices by Hannah Sherman, LCSW

> This workbook provides fun exercises and easy strategies to help kids find focus, develop coping skills, and handle tough situations.

ACKNOWLEDGMENTS

To my four children—Luke, Ben, Sam, and Abby. Thank you for inspiring me every day and encouraging me to slow down and appreciate that the little things in life are really the big things.

Thank you to my fantastic husband, Rick—my proofreader and biggest cheerleader.

Thank you to my amazing parents, Gayl and Chris Sugalski, who have always supported my goals and dreams!

ABOUT THE AUTHOR

LAUREN MOSBACK, LPC, NCC, is a licensed professional counselor and behavior specialist. She specializes in child and adolescent therapy at her practice in the Philadelphia suburbs. Lauren is the author of the award-winning Super Skills series, which includes the picture books *Transforming Anxiety: Grow Resilience and Confidence* and *My Super Skills: Animals and Affirmations*.

Through her books and her counseling work, Lauren helps equip children with tools to understand and manage their emotions and develop self-esteem and resilience. She helps cultivate a strong sense of self-worth in children by helping them explore their unique strengths, values, and coping skills.

For more tips on wellness and managing worry, follow Lauren on Facebook at Empowering Kids Media and @lelise_counselor on Instagram.